Feminist in Pink

A woman's place is in the world

Brenna Stevenson Dilts

Sandee,
your place is
in this world.

To everyone creating a better world
moment by moment.

#feministsinpink #equalityforall

Copyright ©2019 by Brenna Stevenson Dilts

All rights reserved.

I have tried to recreate events, locales, and conversations from my memories of them. In order to maintain their anonymity in some instances I have changed or removed the names of individuals and places. I may have changed some identifying characteristics such as physical properties, occupations and places of residence. Although every effort was made to ensure that the information in this book was correct, I do not assume and hereby disclaims any liability to any party for any loss, damage, or disruption caused by errors or omissions, whether such errors or omissions result from negligence, accident, or any other cause.

Contents

Preface

Feminism has gotten a bad name. It has so many different meanings, connotations, and definitions based on who you ask. Rather than feminism just meaning feminism, many people picture man-hating, radical feminism in which women are seen as superior, rather than equal. I want you to stop for a minute and think about how you define feminism. By definition, it simply means the advocacy for the equality of rights for women. When I think of feminism, I know that is what I mean.

Feminism has its own stereotype. If you ask a random American on the street what they think feminism means, you might hear some story about a woman in cut off shorts, a muscle tee and a short haircut giving some man hating speech about how "I am so tired about being underpaid at work just because I have a set of tits and a vagina." In one conversation, I heard a radical feminist defined in a situation in which a man explained, "... they have a problem with me just because I am a man." I get it, and that is not what I am talking about here. Maybe you find offense to this stereotype. The point is, it is a stereotype. And that is the problem.

I proclaim my belief in feminism because I believe in

women having equal rights and equal opportunities. I also love to get dressed up, wear make-up, get my nails done and have been known to seriously sport some false eyelashes. There are a lot of reasons I am this way including my upbringing, interactions with my extended family, and losing two of the most important people in my life. Experiences continue to influence this belief on a daily basis.

We are living in a world in which we have specific ideas of what it means to be a liberal, conservative, feminist, healthy, sick, a church-goer, or business man. Heck, even the movie *Finding Nemo* displays the prevalence of stereotypes when Marlin is met with, "...you're a clown fish. You're funny, right?"

I have wanted to write this book for over a decade. The irony is that for the longest time I thought this was more of an external belief system; that others see the world as a bunch of opposing standards and beliefs. In reality, I have identified the dichotomous stereotypes around different areas of life because of my tendency to see the world in those two absolute forms, without any variance in between. What we see and believe about ourselves is transferred to what we see and believe about the world. In this book, I share my story and dive into how we can start changing our own ideas around these different prejudices and stereotypes to be more accepting of ourselves and others.

Part One

"It may mean everything, or it may mean nothing. You'll never know until you decide to look at it from a different perspective."

- Unknown

Stereotypes and Gray Areas

I want to live in a world where I can believe in two things that may seem contradictory. I want to live in a world where someone has both liberal and conservative views, is high maintenance and low maintenance, a feminist and a Christian. I want to live in a world of *ands*, not *buts*; a place that indicates that one side is just as real and just as true as the other. One exists separately from the other and does not *not* exist because the other does. I want to live in a world where I can embrace multiple truths at the same time and not have one truth be negated by another. I want to live in a world that moves beyond the stereotypes, prejudices, expectations, and limitations.

For as long as I can remember, I have lived by many sets of rules. On more than one occasion, I have thought to myself, "what is my new rule for that?" I seem to hear an idea, a theory, or a fact and make that a rule; something I can generalize to my whole life. It is not surprising then, that I have wanted to write this book for many years, about what I first thought of as a culture of contradictions. Rather, what I have learned is that there are numerous stereotypes that run rampant in our culture; they drive our views of the world; and for people like me, they become rules that we have to work hard at breaking.

How can we experience multiple, seemingly contradictory, truths inside ourselves and maintain balance? How can we reduce the us-versus-them mentality which separates our world with competition and hate? How can we find the middle ground to respect one another and come up with solutions together? Stephen Schwartz writes in *Wicked*: "There are precious few at ease with moral ambiguities, so we act as if they don't exist." How can we acknowledge that they can and do exist? Is there a way we can promote happiness, love, respect and peace without getting our asses handed to us?

When I first started developing the idea of this book, I described it as a book of "current cultural contradictions." This made sense to me for many years because a contradiction is a statement that implies both the truth and falsity of something.[1] I was looking at the trends of our society such as the prevalence of eating disorders and obesity, and thinking, "those are contradictions." That is true, but it is also true that they

---

[1] Webster Merriam Dictionary (2018). Contradiction. Retrieved May 2, 2018, from https://www.merriam-webster.com/dictionary/contradiction

both exist. Describing the prevalence of both does not get at the foundation of the issue which is that I am a person who frequently sees things at opposite ends of the spectrum and then struggle to see the points in between. It is not enough for this book to be about two contradictory beliefs. It has to look at the root of the problem: Stereotypes and how we develop our beliefs. The purpose of this book is to explore the many, and at times conflicting areas of truth which exist around topics such as mental illness, feminism, health, violence, work ethic and political beliefs. The many truths exist because we have one picture in our mind of what a stereotypical feminist looks like or what a stereotypical sick person looks like, and we ignore the fact that someone may be those things and so much more.

The word *contradictory* may be misleading when discussing these topics, because what may be described as contradictory (e.g., black and white) is in fact a continuum of truths. This book is meant to encourage the acceptance of thoughts and beliefs which seem opposing, and to identify that each holds their own truth. It is meant to encourage the breaking of stereotypical beliefs that hold us and those around us to unrealistic standards.

The more life I live, the more valuable I regard this information and way of being. When I first started dreaming up this book, I was a daughter, cousin, sister, friend, niece; I was many things. I continue to live in the same rural town of 1,300 people where I grew up in. As I write this book now my world has grown. In the years since high school I have become a wife, a motherless and fatherless mother to two young boys, an aunt, a sister-in-law, a daughter-in-law, a godmother, a social worker, an employee and a leader at my current job.

In the last few years, I have observed a select few people in my life start to use the word *and* instead of *but*. It was briefly explained to me that the purpose of this was to show that one thing was not more important or valuable or true than the other; that they both simply existed equally.

Merriam Webster Dictionary describes the word but to be synonymous with the words *unless*, *without*, and *than*. Each of these words indicates that one cannot exist with the other, one only exists if the other does not, and one is greater than the other, respectively.[2] In the book The Achievement Habit, Bernard Roth says, "saying but creates a conflict that does not really exist."[3]

When someone says the word but, what they are implying is that what I am saying - e.g., I am a feminist - is no longer true because of something else - I like the gender-stereotypical color pink. What that person is saying is that I cannot possibly be a real feminist because I do not look, act, or think, like a feminist should, or like the right color that fits their version of what a feminist should like. We have got to stop

---

[2] Merriam Webster Dictionary (2018). And. Retrieved from https://www.merriam-webster.com/dictionary/and

[3] Roth, Bernard (2015). The achievement habit: stop wishing, start doing, and take command of your life. New York, NY: Harper Collins Publishing

shoulding on ourselves and others.

There are many parts of me that seem contradictory due to the stereotypes that are in place. For example, some might say the stereotypical feminist is a lesbian with short hair, wearing no make-up, that hates men. When one thinks of a person believing in equal rights and opportunities for women, they tend not to picture a woman who enjoys wearing makeup, getting her hair highlighted, and playing into the ideals of beauty because she likes the way it makes her feel. I embody those qualities and I am a feminist; I also do not fit into the socially constructed stereotype of a feminist. I suspect this is true for many others out there as well.

This book is about stating that I can be a feminist and I can wear makeup and love the color pink. It is about removing the lines from stereotypes and expectations we set upon ourselves and those around us. This book is about prejudices and helping reduce them in ourselves and others. It is about accepting that we live in a world where we can form our own opinions, beliefs, and truths and that does not mean that someone else's opinions, beliefs and truths, are any less real or valuable than the next persons.

Consider for a minute the difference when someone says the word *and*, rather than the word *but*. When someone says and they are making a connecting between two truths. The word *and* means a connection or addition especially of items within the same class or type —used to join sentence elements of the same grammatical rank or function; and is used as a function word to express logical modification, consequence, antithesis, or supplementary explanation. Ironically, the Merriam-Webster Dictionary puts the words *but* and *and* together in exemplifying a conjunction, meaning a word that joins together words, phrases, or clauses of equal importance."[4] To say that the word but is a conjunction that joins two things of equal importance is a direct contradiction to other definitions of the word *but*, in that it joins together two unequal words.

Contradictions do have their place in this world. Meredith Narissi, expresses how without contradictions, dance would not be possible:

> In dance you use contrast. You leap by first pressing down. In belly dance, you may push the ball of your foot into the floor to lift your hip. You might lower your shoulder as you raise your arm. You shimmy your hips at one-hundred shimmies per second while your arms float up at a barely perceptible pace. You travel in a circle to come to know center. You surrender to the not-knowing in order to know. You live in both realms, the material and the spiritual. Unseen forces of the mysterious realm intersect on this plane. They affect your life. You see how nothing really happens without the mysterious unseen forces.... You learn to speak your truth and express your story. The mouth is between the head and the

[4] Merriam Webster Dictionary (2019) Conjunction. Retrieved from hppts://www.merriam-webster.com/dictionary/conjuction.

> heart. You find harmony between mind and emotion. Your story becomes your truth.[5]

The distinction between the words *and* and *but* is important to me. If I continually think I am a feminist, but I like to feel pretty, I can drive myself into a downward spiral of shame about who I am and what I believe. If I say I am a feminist, but so is Judy and she is so much more of a feminist than me because she does not care about beauty standards, I (1) reiterate the idea that feminists can only look, act and believe one way, and (2) take away my own power and self-worth. Boo.

The idea of seemingly contradictory views or opinions can also be applied when considering views between two people. When this is done, it is important to consider perspective. Perspective is the exact thing that allows us to see that two sides can be two truths, and one is not incorrect because the other exists. Consider a cartoon with two individuals arguing whether they are viewing a 6 or a 9 - both are correct as they are standing on different sides of the number. Or think of the sun - on one side of the world, a person is viewing a sunset and on the other, a sunrise.

Conflicting thoughts, feelings, and ideas can occur between two people or within one person's mind. When one person experiences inconsistent thoughts or

---

[5] Narissi, M. Z. (2017) Mystical secrets of a feminine path to enlightenment. Bloomington, IN: Balboa Press.

attitudes, it is called cognitive dissonance.[6] Cognitive dissonance often feels like discomfort. Considering this, it is no surprise that I, for one, hate when this happens. Perhaps that is why this book has been so important to me. I have had very interesting experiences that have led to conflicting emotions and ways of being. In some ways, I am a stereotypical social worker, entering the field after personal experiences lead me to search for answers. In other ways, I am not. I struggle with balancing between identifying my emotions and leaning into them and wanting to (read: absolutely) run in the other direction. I tend not to do anything in moderation. Moderation is an avoidance of extremes in one's actions, beliefs, or habits; not violent, severe, or intense.[7] I am a one-or-the-other, all-or-nothing, balls-to-the-walls type of woman.

This book is about gray areas; accepting multiple truths and discouraging the word but which says two seemingly conflicting beliefs cannot both be true. It is about embracing the differences inside you that go against the stereotypes and expectations of society. It is about embracing and honoring the differences between each of us.

What I am suggesting is that the age-old phrase, "you can't have your cake and eat it too," is inaccurate. We

---

[6] Festinger, L. (1957). A theory of cognitive dissonance. Palo Alto, CA: Stanford University Press.

[7] Merriam Webster Dictionary (2018). Moderation. Retrieved from https://www.merriam-webster.com/thesaurus/moderation

can have the best of both worlds. While we may not be able to have our cake in our hands and eat it at the same point in time, eating our cake does not negate the fact that we did get to enjoy our time when we actually had our cake.

Finally, I leave you with this thought by Katie Willcox, author of *Healthy is the New Skinny*:

> You have the ability to fully display beauty apart from vanity, influence apart from manipulation, style apart from materialism, kindness apart from passivity, strength apart from competition, and dignity without degradation.[8]

---

[8] Willcox, Katie (2017). Healthy is the new skinny: Your guide to self-love in a "picture perfect" world. Carlsbad, CA: Hay House Publishing.

Part Two

"Perspective is the way we see things when we look at them from a certain distance, and it allows us to appreciate their true value"

-Rafael E. Pino

Black and White

I am a chronic black and white thinker. You might know the type; maybe you are the type. I have difficulty bending rules and making exceptions. I struggle with the inflexibility of routines and processes – and speaking of rules and processes, they are kind of my thing. I believe we want simplicity and predictability. Therefore, we want things to be this or that, good or bad, healthy or unhealthy.

There are many benefits to my laser-like focus on right versus wrong, rules, processes, and lines in the sand. For example, I work in Quality Assurance as a supervisor. I am someone who assists with ensuring compliance to rules, regulations, and standards. It could not be a better fit really because my t's and i's are crossed, dotted and then quadruple-checked. My degree is in clinical social work which surprises most people. It is not because I am not compassionate or kind; I just tend to be a bit rigid. I started my work as a clinician doing case management work and then outpatient therapy. I struggled daily with the lack of rules, lines, structure and completed to do list items. The idea of a prescribed amount of therapy to cure someone's struggle is incomplete and naive. Ironically, I worked with several clients who also struggled with black-and-white thinking and I was constantly talking about how to "live in the gray." Making the move to quality assurance was one of the best decisions of my life. While my preference for structure and rules can be beneficial, some days, it can bring a storm of problems. I swear this happens more often than not.

As an incessant black and white thinker, it is imperative that I expand my capacity to accept the many contradictory thoughts and beliefs of myself and others by living in the gray and using the word *and* instead of the word *but*.

Growing up, I received contradictory advice about when to speak up and when not to. I was the middle child of an older sister and a younger brother. Perhaps my struggle with living in the gray comes from being in the middle of my siblings and my parents; you know, common middle child problems.

I remember one particular evening we were at some sport ceremony for one of my siblings. I was sitting in between my parents and was pretty sure I was going to starve to death if I had to sit there any longer listening to the boring ceremony and not getting anything to eat. (I am now learning about myself that I need to listen quickly when my body says, "eat" if I don't want to turn into a hangry monster.) I started whining, and I do not even remember what it was exactly that I was whining about. I do remember my mom saying to me, “this isn’t the place to start complaining,” and my dad saying, “Beth, she can say whatever she wants, whenever she wants.” It was almost as though I had an angel in white and devil in red on each shoulder. I see that time, when I was a 12 or maybe 14-year-old girl, as the time that black or white thinking truly took hold of my brain. That sounds much simpler than it actually is. It is not as though that one point in time was the cause of a life’s worth of polarized thought. Rather, it is my first recollected memory of creating a rule about being outspoken as either good or bad, instead of multiple shades of gray.

While researching this book and what it might mean to “live in the gray,” imagine my surprise in Googling “living in the gray.” There are countless search results including songs, religious beliefs, therapeutic techniques, and self-help books. The list goes on and on like the song “*The Song That Never End*” from the kids’ show, *Lamb Chop*.

In the song “Living in the Gray” by Godsmack:

> Not everything is always black or white
> Sometimes we're living in the gray
> Controlling every way, for your own identity
> No room for mistakes, and preaching your hypocrisy
> Maybe one day you'll come to realize that
> That all you do and say was meant to be in the

> gray
> Not everything is always black or white
> Sometimes we're living in the gray.[9]

That is what I am talking about. It is about giving up control, making mistakes, and bending the rules.

Despite my undergraduate education in psychology and graduate education in social work, it took until I was about eight hours into writing this book and ten years into thinking about it to realize that maybe not everyone struggles with this black-and-white thinking like I do. At the same time, I would be hard-pressed to believe that there is someone out there without a single stigmatizing or stereotypical belief.

In Gretchen Ruben's book *The Four Tendencies*,[10] she asserts that people have one of four personality tendencies:

> Upholder: "I do what others expect of me—and what I expect from myself."
>
> Questioner: "I do what I think is best, according to my judgment. If it doesn't make sense, I won't do it."
>
> Obliger: "I do what I have to do. I don't want to let others down, but I may let myself down."

---

[9] Erna, S., Larkin, S., Merrill, R., and Rombola, T. (2014). Living in the gray. [Recorded by Godsmack]. On *1000HP*. New York, NY: republic Records

[10] Ruben, G. (2017). The four tendencies. New York, NY: Penguin Random House.

> Rebel: "I do what I want, in my own way. If you try to make me do something—even if I try to make myself do something—I'm less likely to do it."

Knowing that someone has written an entire book about whether we do or do not break rules, leads me to believe that I am not the only one who engages in stereotyping or rule-making behaviors.

Maybe, like the idea of living in the gray, there is a continuum on which you fall in your ability to embrace gray thinking. This may be the difference black-and-white thinking as a cognitive distortion that leads to a mental illness or struggles, or not. Maybe we also move to different places on the continuum based on who we are spending time with, if we accidentally burned our toast that morning, if we missed our morning workout, if a friend cancels plans or a number of other factors on any given day. I have been privileged to experience a variety of cultures and to have parents that generated relationships deep in my community, introducing me to many different people. I have learned that some people are able to make better judgment calls based on a full review of the information available to them.

For example, if three people - let's say A, B, and C - are all told the following: New studies have shown that eating 1,200 calories a day will guarantee significant weight loss with lasting results; the 1,200 calories should be a combination of 20% protein, 50% carbohydrates and 30% fat; this should be combined with drinking one gallon of water per day. Person A takes this information and adds in their preferences, experiences, possibilities of snacking between meals and enjoying birthday cake if they go to a party. After she considers the information, she moderately follows the plan proposed to her while accepting the times when she does not follow the plan without remorse. Person A is high on the gray thinking scale as she does not consider the plan as an absolute to follow or not follow.

Person B receives the same information and continues to ask for extreme clarification and "what-if" scenarios (e.g., what if I go to a birthday party? Is it okay if I eat 29% fats and 21% protein? Do I get a break if I am on vacation?). Person B also chooses to follow the meal plan and feels pretty good about it. He frequently weighs all the options and reassures himself when exceptions should be made. Person B is somewhere in the middle of the gray thinking scale.

Person C receives the information and either rushes into a decision or avoids the decision at all saying, "forget it, I will never stick with this plan!". If he is able to make the decision, he thinks he has to be either right or wrong; he must follow the plan 100% of the time and ensure he sticks with the macronutrient breakdowns exactly, or the whole thing is a bust. He fails to realize that different factors may need to be accounted for at different times. He does not see any room for mistakes, error or judgment. He feels crappy about himself because no matter how hard he tries, he can't possibly comply 100% and although the expectation is unrealistic, he views it as a personal flaw, as somehow representative of his morality. Person C is engaging in black and white thinking, also termed polarized thinking, which classifies as a cognitive distortion.

I have slowly started moving my way up the gray scale from constant black and white thinking, to significantly increasing my ability to consider a bit grayer. I wish I could say I am always high on the gray scale now, but those cognitive distortions still creep in.

Cognitive distortions were first described in literature by psychiatrist Aaron Beck in 1976. Beck described them as maladaptive ways of viewing oneself and the world. He proposed that cognitive distortions lead to negative emotions and problematic behaviors. Cognitive distortions are part of a larger treatment theory called Cognitive Therapy which addresses emotional disorders such as depression through therapy. Cognitive therapy helps clients look at the distortions and address how to reverse the irrational and psychologically harmful biases behind them. [11]

In 1980, psychiatrist David Burns identified ten common cognitive distortions that are best known today, including polarized thinking.[12] This type of thinking is also referred to as dichotomous, all-or-nothing, or black-and-white thinking that we have been exploring here. This type of irrational thought distortion is viewing

---

[11] Beck, A. T. (1976). *Cognitive therapies and emotional disorders*. New York: New American Library.

[12] Burns, D. D. (1980). *Feeling good: The new mood therapy*. New York, NY, USA: Signet.

something as either-or, without considering the full spectrum and range of possibilities. Further, it combines these absolute truths with moral superiority in which, if I do this, I am good and if I do not, I am bad. Those rules I have frequently made for myself were very much connected to morality. If my clothing is not folded perfectly or hung in a color coordinated order – yes, I really used to do that – I told myself I was bad/stupid/incapable.

It is not surprising, that individuals with distorted thought processes have been found to be at a higher risk of experiencing symptoms of mental illness such as depression.[13] If we look at the examples of people A, B, and C and the weight loss plan, person C who engages in black and white thinking is likely to feel great failure when not meeting that 100% goal.

Cognitive distortions may occur with differing frequency depending on the individual's core beliefs, which fall on the sociotropy-autonomy scale. The sociotropy-autonomy scale was developed by Aaron Beck as an indicator of the social determinant factors that correlate with an individual's cognitive effects on depressive symptoms.

Sociotrophy is an individual's excessive investment in interpersonal relationships out of a strong need for social acceptance. These tendencies can cause the individual to be overly nurturing towards people with

---

[13] Rnic, K., Dozois, D. J. A., & Martin, R. A. (2016). Cognitive distortions, humor styles, and depression. *Europe's Journal of Psychology*, 12(3): 348-362. doi:10.5964/cjop.v12i3.1118

whom they do not have close relationships. Beck added three areas to the sociotrophy scale, Concern About Disapproval, Concern About Separation, and Pleasing Others.[14]

Autonomy describes an individual's tendency to place value in their individual achievements and separation from other people. The specific areas of autonomy, according to Beck are: Individualistic or Autonomous Achievement, Freedom from Control of Others, and Preference for Solitude. According to Beck's cognitive theory of depression, if an individual experiences high interpersonal concerns, they are at higher risk for depression when interpersonal stressors, are experienced.[15]

In other words, if you are trying to stick to a weight loss plan and you care deeply about what other people think about your compliance to the plan and your ability to lose weight, and you fail, you are more likely to experience depressive symptoms than someone who experiences low interpersonal concern. This becomes even more likely when you fall higher on the sociotrophy scale and engage in polarized thinking. The important part to take away is that when you place a great deal of value on what other people think, and you engage in

---

[14] Beck, A. T., et al. (1983). *Development of the sociotropy-autonomy scale: A measure of personality factors in psychopathology*. Unpublished manuscript. Philadelphia: University of Pennsylvania.

[15] Westmaas, L.J., Ference, R., and Wild, C.T. (2006). Autonomy (vs. sociotropy) and depressive symptoms in quitting smoking: Evidence for trait-congruence and the role of gender. *Addictive Behavior, 31 (10):* 1744-60.

black and white thinking, you are at an even higher risk for depressive symptoms. That alone is a reason to try to embrace the gray.

In an article on cognitive distortions, Summer Beretsky presents a short activity to better understand polarized or black-and-white thinking.[16] She instructs readers to review a list of 15 coupled contradictory words (e.g., black and white; large and small; up and down; good and bad; happy and sad; calm and anxious) then write down a single word that describes the middle ground between each pair of opposites.

It can be tricky to find a word that describes the middle between those words. Eventually, they might start to look the same. The first couple are relatively easy: gray, medium, middle. As you start to near the bottom, you may start to struggle with finding those moderating words. However, when someone asks how you are feeling and you have been feeling slightly anxious but mostly content and answer "anxious" anyway, it can alter the truth of how you are feeling.

We have the option to explain, and therefore, remember experiences how we choose. Exaggerating our feelings or experiences by describing or thinking of them as black and white with only two options, can alter how we perceive, remember, and experience our life. If we

---

[16] Beretsky, S. (2009). Cognitive distortion: how does black-and-white thinking hurt us? Psych Central. Retrieved on February 26, 2018, from https://psychcentral.com/blog/cognitive-distortion-how-does-black-and-white-thinking-hurt-us/

constantly choose to select the exaggerated negative, we will begin to see a pattern of negativity in our lives. As Madisyn Taylor writes, "it is the story we tell ourselves about what happens that makes all the difference such as when someone does not fit in the stereotypical mold we are trying to put them in."[17]

Confirmation bias may be another way in which we further fall into dichotomous thinking. Confirmation bias is a type of cognitive bias identified in 1960 by Peter Wason. Research on cognitive biases has suggested that cognitive biases aid in decision making by generalizing one situation to similar situations. Additionally, it has shown that humans engage in these behaviors based on different heuristics, or cognitive biases. Heuristics are mental shortcuts that we as humans take to help us come to conclusions more quickly. While heuristics can certainly help us to come to conclusions more quickly than if we had to weigh all potential outcomes, they can also lead to systematic and predictable errors.[18]

Specifically, confirmation bias, is seeking and accepting information that confirms your existing belief and disregarding information that is inconsistent with your beliefs.[19] Confirmation biases impact how people gather

---

[17] Taylor, M. (2018). Create a supportive life story. *Daily OM*. Retrieved on November 7, 2018 from https://www.dailyom.com/cgi-bin/display/articledisplay.cgi?aid=68411

[18] Wason, P. C. (1960). On the failure to eliminate hypotheses in a conceptual task. Quarterly Journal of Experimental Psychology, 12: 129-140.

[19] Kahneman, D.; Tversky, A. (1972). "Subjective probability: A judgment of representativeness". *Cognitive Psychology*, 3 (3): 430-454.

information, but they also influence how we interpret and recall information. For example, people who support or oppose a particular issue will not only seek information that supports their opinions; they will also interpret news stories in a way that upholds their existing ideas.

If you have engaged in black-and-white thinking resulting in rules (e.g., I cannot ever voice my opinion in public or I must always voice my opinion in public), you will continue to search for examples that will support your rule. Thankfully, Tversky and Kahneman concluded that an awareness and understanding of cognitive biases could improve their use for decision-making to result in fewer errors. In other words, now that you know that your mind may be using confirmation bias to further your belief in the rules you have set for yourself, you can begin to question those beliefs and start to search for other information that may help you make more moderate decisions. As Summer Beretsky says,

> Catching yourself using black and white thinking (and correcting yourself) can transform an unrealistic thought into a more truthful (and probably less stress-inducing) one. Unglamorous adjectives like "middle-aged" or "in-between" and low-impact phrases like "moderately shy" probably won't win you any grand literary awards, but they do stand a good chance at helping you view the world through a more

accurate lens.[20]

It is important to know that if you engage in a black-and-white cognitive distortion, you are at a higher risk for depression and other symptoms of mental illness (e.g., anxiety). If you highly regard others' opinions, you are at an even greater risk. Our thinking can be our own worst enemy. There is no causation here. It is not to say if you engage in black and white thinking that you will absolutely experience symptoms of depression, or that you will have poor self-confidence. I have found those things to be true in my personal experience and would be remiss to not share something that might help you too.

Not only have studies shown that black and white thinking can be detrimental to mental health, but studies have shown that individuals with more frequent cognitive distortions tend to have lower general health, defined as the state of physical, mental and social wellbeing.[21]

Perhaps one of my favorite anti-polarized thought sayings is, "Do no harm and take no shit."[22] Over the

---

[20] Beretsky, S. (2009). Cognitive distortion: how does black-and-white thinking hurt us? Psych Central. Retrieved on February 26, 2018, from https://psychcentral.com/blog/cognitive-distortion-how-does-black-and-white-thinking-hurt-us/

[21] Samadifard, H.R., and Narimani M. (2017). The role of cognitive belief, fusion and distortion in predicting the general health of couples. J Community Health Research, 6(3): 132 40

[22] Nascimento, G. (2016). Do no harm, but take no shit; A simple philosophy. *A New Kind of Human*. Retrieved from https://anewkindofhuman.com/no-harm-take-no-shit/

years, I have talked time and time again about how I wanted to write this book. I talked about how I was the exact example of why seemingly contradictory ideas should be accepted for one person. Unfortunately, I have let the black and white thinking take over my life more times than I can count. I have found it to be true that when I engage in constant polarized thought, I tend to be at my worst. I have used that thinking for good and bad, and it has affected my own life and the lives of others.

We are constantly inundated with sayings, phrases, quotes, and empowerment speeches. When I type "self-help books" into the books category of Amazon, I get over 700,000 search results. Searching it through Google gets me over 155,000,000 results. That is just seeking self-help. It does not include the "help" we get when we are not even asking for it. Advertisements on television, social media, and the pop-ups that interrupt your favorite, mindless game on your phone; friends sharing words of wisdom when you are venting your latest frustration; and training received at work. We hear "don't be bothered by what anyone thinks of you" while we see many examples of, "if you want to be cool, fit in and belong you must wear __, look like __, eat __, and watch __." This can lead to some of the worst polarization.

I am notorious for reading a book or watching a video and making that my life's mission for the next 2 days, 2 weeks, 2 months or until the next life-altering idea becomes my next life's mission. In some ways, this can be positive. As I write this book, I am approaching a year of self-exploration in which I have read countless books and explored ways in which I can become more vulnerable, more empathetic, less know-it-all-y, make more connections, and learn to consider all people as people. That is surely, positive, right? Kind of.

Black and white thinking can lead to compulsive behaviors, because to think one way is to behave one way. How boring does that sound? Beyond that, compulsiveness is like multiple sets of rules. I will always act vulnerable, empathetic, humble, and kind and if I do not, I have failed. Feelings of failure lead to feelings of depression. Beyond that, who wants to watch someone else be "perfect" all the time? I recognized it in others before I was able to recognize it in myself: watching someone else do things "perfectly" is exhausting and intimidating. It makes you want to not connect with those people; avoid them really. If in my efforts to connect and be vulnerable and be kind, I am judging myself for my failures, I am inadvertently judging others for their failures and therefore counteracting what I am trying to do in the first place.

I have done this with countless pieces of advice, literature, advertisement messages, sermons at church and standards at work. It is almost laughable. I think back about how I have made all-or-nothing thinking and behaving my entire life. If I am going to do something, I will be the best at it. When I decided senior year of high school that I was going to be in a high school musical, I did not just audition for any role; I went for and acted as Cinderella. When I wanted to be on the yearbook staff, I did not just write a few articles; I became one of the two editors.

Yes, those experiences are positive. However, this "be the best" mindset also affected me negatively. When I could not be the best, I would not participate. I loved running. I ran one year on the middle school track and field team and when my times were significantly slower than everyone else, and I placed second to last or on the worst days of my life (ha!), last, I was broken and vowed to not race again. I will add, however, that I did race again in my adult life in 5K, 10K, 10 mile and half marathon races. So maybe there is hope after all.

When I trained, I found the races to be miserable, because I was constantly comparing myself to others and expecting more and more and more of myself. When I did not train, I could see nothing but how amazing it was that I could even complete such a race. One year in college, I was running 3 miles every single day and eating the same breakfasts (half a grapefruit), lunches – (a miniscule amount of cheddar cheese and an apple), and dinners (homemade pita chips, 2 tablespoons of hummus, and a handle of grapes). (More on the body image shitstorm later.)

Even as I write this book, I realize that I am compulsively writing. I spend every free moment I am not picking boogers from my kids' faces, exercising to stay sane, or working my good old 8-5, opening up this document, typing out stories and researching studies and information to explain why I am the way I am.

How can you avoid black-and-white thinking and acting? Be gracious. Be gracious to yourself and be gracious to others. And when you have not yet perfected being gracious 100% of the time, give yourself some more grace.

Happy and Sad

When I think about the words happy and sad, I think about the day my dad died. It has taken me many losses and years of therapy to realize that I could and absolutely needed to be able to experience more than one emotion at a time. In fact, it is part of human nature and good mental health to do so.

When I was fourteen years old, I was sitting in the living room of the house I grew up in waiting for my best friend and our respective boyfriends to pick me up to go bowling. My parents came and sat with me; my mom on the coffee table in front of me and my dad on the couch. They said they needed to talk to me and they both started crying. My mom said, "your dad is sick. He has 'ALS'." I remember being confused; I had no idea what 'ALS' was or how it was going to affect my family. From the pure grief my parents were exhibiting, I could tell it was not a good thing and I began to cry too. I don't know if they actually explained to me that day or not that by getting the diagnosis of ALS, my dad was receiving a life sentence and a grim prognosis.

I remember asking, “who knows?” My mom explained that my sister did and that some teachers at school in case I needed the support. At the time, I did not think twice about that response. Through years of therapy, I came to realize how mad I was that other adults were told about my dad’s terrible diagnosis before me; that I felt betrayed and left out, and that it was okay to feel those things, along with sadness, confusion, empathy, and fear.

I asked my parents if I needed to stay home or if I was still able to go, and they encouraged me to continue to live life. After we talked, they continued to cry so I found it necessary to also cry. What person would sit there and let their parents cry, but not in fact also find the news sad? (The answer to that is someone who had no idea what the enormity of that news would mean.) I let them be and went and found my sister in her room. We laid in bed and cried, though I don’t remember if I even knew his prognosis at that time. Or maybe I did, and I blocked it out.

I went bowling shortly thereafter and explained that my family had received some bad news, and my dad was sick. I remember laying my head on my best friend’s shoulder in the back of her boyfriend’s car. I don’t remember any more about that day.

As time went on, I learned more and more about ALS, or amyotrophic lateral sclerosis. Some know it better as Lou Gehrig's disease. If you are lucky, you have never heard of this disease, nor know anyone it has affected. It is an ugly disease. ALS is a progressive neurological disorder which results in damage to the spinal cord, causing neurons to die and preventing messages from getting to the muscles, eventually causing the muscles to waste away, and the hardening of the spinal cord in advanced ALS. This all happens as its victims tend to remain cognitively aware. It's about as fun as it sounds.

Throughout high school, I wrote a couple of papers on the disease. I am someone who likes to know everything – particularly facts and what the future might entail. Sometimes I feel this is a curse. When it came to knowing the inevitability of my dad's horrendous death, it was definitely one of those times.

I remember watching the movie *Jenifer*, about a woman with ALS. I was drawn to it because ALS was and still is such a rare disease that most people had no idea what I was dealing with. I was searching for a way to feel connected or perhaps understood. The movie was terrible. I do not remember most of it, but I remember when Jenifer's disease had progressed and she wanted to end her life, a nurse said, "how are you planning to do that? Your hands don't work so you can't tie a rope or pull a trigger. Your neck and throat muscles are weak, so you can't swallow pills. And you can no longer walk so drowning yourself in a lake is out of the question." What a thing to remember about a movie, and to consider in the future life of a family member. Rather than helping me feel connected, it left me feeling even sadder and more confused.

Somewhere shortly after my dad was diagnosed, I learned that the prognosis of the disease was somewhere between three and five years. My parents were committed to "beating it." They read books, switched to all organic food, took yoga, and said "I love you" every time we parted, like it might be the last. When I would get sad about my dad dying, my mom would say, "you never know, I could go first. I could go out and get hit by a bus tomorrow." We would all laugh because that could not possibly happen.

Three years came and went. In that time, I had countless trips to the therapist to deal with the grief that I did not quite understand – or perhaps did not even admit to myself I was experiencing. Maybe I just thought it was irony that I began experiencing symptoms of depression shortly after his diagnosis. Most likely the grief combined with my increased risk for struggles with mental illness due to family history was the cause for my emotional shit storm. Or maybe it was hormones, though I doubt the latter. I remember feeling mad and then thinking it probably was not okay to feel mad because I was wasting good time I had left with him. He was so positive and did not want to talk about his imminent death. He was all about making our time count.

Four years after his diagnosis, he took me to Wyoming on a hunting trip. Each of us siblings got to go on a trip with him one on one. My younger brother and I got hunting trips and my sister got a trip to the Mall of America. I felt a little cheated because while I bragged about how cool it was that I shot a mule deer and an antelope, I was a little sad I didn't get the shopping trip. My dad was doing the best he could to relate to each of us, and perhaps it was my own fault for not telling him for years that I did not like hunting, that it in fact made me very sad. That the turkeys I shot and the deer I killed out west were adventures I went on purely to be able to spend time with him, and I did not think he would love me or accept me for who I was. That trip to Wyoming was the last hunting I ever did.

That fall, my mom started getting sick. She was losing weight really quickly, and was not a big woman to begin with. The doctors did not know what was wrong with her. For the first couple of months, I thought she had an eating disorder. I was mad at her. I was with her in her walk-in closet one day and said, "jeez mom, eat a stick of butter or something." I do not remember exactly what she said in response, but my comment was met with something along the lines of, "this isn't my fault Brenna!" She spent the majority of the last eight months of her life in and out of the hospital.

I continued to go to college and believe that she would be okay. It was not possible that I would have two parents with a terminal illness, was it? My mom had this friend that called me one day and told me how serious this was; that I needed to leave school and return home to my parents. I was furious with her. My parents continued to tell me that everything would be fine and that wasn't necessary. When I told my mom about her friend's call, she said that was ridiculous and that she would say something. I returned home for the summer and I noticed she was getting smaller and smaller by the day.

That June, my grandmother passed away, and I remember sitting on my mom's lap and crying. There I was, 19 years old, sitting on my mom's lap and crying. A few days later, my dad called out in the night, "Brenna, help!" My mom was sitting on the toilet, pale skin and shaking from pain. My dad was so weak by this time that he could not get her to the car, and it was clear she needed medical attention.

In the small, rural town we live in we can drive to the hospital faster than an ambulance could get to our house and back to the hospital. She probably weighed a hundred pounds; I lifted her right up and ran with her to the car. When I got to the hospital, she was still shaking from the pain. I remember being furious at the nurses, at the doctors, at the situation. From what I can remember, they couldn't find her in their electronic health system to see the medications she was on and therefore weren't getting her drugs fast enough to ease her pain. She lay in the hospital bed crying, shaking, moaning, and repeating, "it hurts." My dad was yelling, and I felt helpless.

The next day while visiting her in the hospital, I walked in the room, and she smiled and greeted me by saying, "there's my superhero." Then one hot day in July, just eight months after I noticed she was getting ill, days after carrying her to the car, she died. In those eight months, she was treated for vascular lymphoma and vasculitis, and experienced a stroke, a heart attack, and finally failure of all her organs. So, there you have it. She said she could go first, and she did. I was mad, I was sad, I was confused, and I hurt.

I remember watching my dad sobbing at her bedside, begging her to stay and saying he would go instead. My dad was always a strong man. He did not cry until the first time I saw him in the hospital eight years before my mom's death. At that time, he had had an appendectomy that got infected and left him in the hospital for two weeks. My grandmother took me to visit him. Upon walking into his hospital doorway, I cried. There was my tough, stubborn, not in the least bit sedentary dad laying hooked up to machines in a hospital bed. He cried too. When we left, my grandmother referenced my tears and said, "you shouldn't have done that; you need to be strong for him." In that short sentence, I learned, if you are strong, you do not cry, you are not sad. Watching my parents, I learned that if you want to be positive you do not talk about the sad truth of death and dying, and you pretend everything is fine.

After my mom died, our family fell apart. I took off to New York to stay with my aunt, uncle, and two young cousins in Brooklyn. I did everything I could to take care of myself the best way I knew how. I worked out at Bikram yoga, cycling, running, anything to focus on my body instead of my emotions.

I stayed away for eight weeks. I was stuck in this weird place of feeling obligated to move home to care for my dying father and 16-year-old brother, despite knowing how detrimental that would be to my mental health. At the end of the summer, I did go home. I took a semester off from my college course and did my best as a nineteen-year-old to grocery shop, cook, clean and work full-time. And it never felt like enough. I remember my dad berating me one day for not doing anything for them. I was crying, obviously upset because to me, staying home from college and not pursuing my dreams was the ultimate sacrifice. He turned around within five minutes and asked me to help him put his shoes on.

Writing this now, I realize how impossible it must have felt for him as well. Here he was, this strong, independent man. He moved out of his house at 16, built a successful business and provided for his family and was then watching it all be taken away; from my mom, to his body. At the time though, I felt nothing but anger. Anger that he dare say I did not do anything for him and then ask me to do something for him. I went back to school the next semester. I could not have possibly stayed there any longer.

Shortly before graduating a few years later, I met my now-husband. I was in the process of applying to grad schools all over the country. At one point, I remember talking to my mom about how and where I would pursue my educational dreams, and she told me to never let her or my dad's illness hold me back. In considering graduate school, I kept my late mother's advice in mind. I ended up being accepted out of state, but I decided to move to my hometown and pursue my degree online in order to be closer to my dad and continue to pursue a relationship with my husband.

I moved in with my dad for a few weeks but that proved

impossible. I desperately wanted to be the daughter that could give up everything and do nothing but be a caregiver for my dad. But I wasn't that daughter. I was the type of daughter who could be close by but needed my own space. I needed to care for myself. And now that I am honest with myself, I realize could not stand to see my dad as ill as he was 24 hours a day.

The events that led up to the last few weeks of my dad's life are now fuzzy. I know he was in and out of the hospital, and we worked quickly to get an attorney to the hospital to complete a will. I remember asking over and over, "how much time do we have?" and never getting more than, "we don't know, but not long."

The last time he was in the hospital, we found out he had an intestinal blockage. The doctors said he was too ill to operate on, and my dad made the decision to go home and die. Of course, he never said that. He had withered away to barely nothing and was difficult to understand, but he said "PMA," meaning positive mental attitude, time and time again. He didn't want us to cry or be sad.

At a time when your only parent left is dying and is asking you not to cry, it is confusing. To feel like you have to constantly fight back tears and stay strong is exhausting. Somehow, we did it. He was in hospice care, "staying comfortable," for nearly three weeks. We had nearly 20 family members in and out of the house in rotating shifts and caring for him in his last days.

There were funny moments. During his last weeks, he was difficult to understand. At one point, I was sitting in his room with him when our rooster began to crow repeatedly outside. My dad - literally on his deathbed - said, “boy that rooster has a lot of confidence.” Another time he was trying to tell me something by going through the alphabet for each letter. He would nod on the letters he wanted. After about 6 letters of complete nonsense, he smiled and said, “I’m just fucking with you.” Sometimes, the positivity wasn’t all that bad.

There were beautiful moments. One of the most beautiful moments in my life was when a friend of ours brought his guitar over and played music in our living room. My dad sat in his chair with his eyes closed, surrounded by many friends and family, and it was beautiful.

It was not many days later that I was painting my nails, and my aunt came and found me and told me, “it happened.” I was standing in the laundry room. She hugged me, and I did not cry. I said, “right now?” and when she nodded, I said, “okay.” I ate lasagna. It is a weird thing. I did not feel sad; I felt nothing. When my mom died, I remember lying in bed crying so hard, my heart so broken and hurting more than any pain I had ever experienced, questioning how I would ever move on.

I could not even drop a tear the day my dad died. I did not cry at his funeral. It has taken many years and many therapy sessions to finally figure out that I was relieved and a bit ashamed the day he died. I was ashamed that I did not do more, that I did not say more and that I was not a better daughter. I was ashamed because I was so relieved that the “dying” part of my dad’s life was finally over. It was ten years. He survived with ALS for ten years before it took his life. That is a long time to sit around and wait for someone to die. Now when I think about it, I think, "Of course I was relieved!" The man was stubborn, and man did he hold on to life for a long time. Much longer than anyone expected. I was not relieved that he was no longer here, but I was relieved that he was (and we were) not suffering through him dying anymore.

I walked around angry for years after that. I could not identify any other feelings regarding his death; just anger. I told my mom once in high school how mad I was, and she told me to be mad at God because he could handle it. After my dad died, I wasn't mad at God. I didn't even know if I believed in God. I was a classic case of, "how is there a God if something so awful can happen? And if there is a God and he did that, I don't want him." Shortly after his death, my aunt asked me how I was feeling, and I said, "angry." I was not able to identify feelings of sadness or relief, only feelings of anger.

It is ironic, really. I started learning about the five stages of grief when I was in high school and processing my dad's diagnosis. Elisabeth Kübler-Ross presented the five stages of grief in her book *On Death and Dying.*[23] Kübler-Ross suggested there are five stages of grief: denial, anger, bargaining, depression, and acceptance. She further proposed that these stages are not linear and are

[23] Kubler-Ross (1997). On death and dying. New York, NY: Simon & Schuster, Inc.

unique to each person experiencing them. For someone who expects all aspects of life to be black and white and fit into neat emotional boxes, this is a complicated concept.

When I consider the stages of grief now, I realize that I experienced each of these with my mother's death, clearly and quickly. By the end of the summer, I had a dream of her one night. It was black everywhere, and I couldn't see anything. All I could sense was hearing her voice say, "it's alright, Brenna. I'm okay." If you read that and thought, "yeah right," I am with you. I do not really believe in spirits or a connection to the afterlife, and yet it brought me comfort.

The two years prior to my mother's death, she began exploring her abilities to connect with the afterlife. It creeped me out. She told me that I had the ability and I could explore it with her, and I gave her a resounding, "no."

Regardless, somehow in that dream I experienced peace and acceptance.

With my dad's death, the stages of grief were a bit more complicated. I grieved for ten years over my dad's death while he was still alive on this earth. I grieved the shit out of that loss, and frankly, I think I was over it. One stage that should be added to the stages of grief is shame. Not that I'm suggesting we should feel shame, but rather than it is likely a natural emotion during the grieving process. I did not do enough, I did not say enough, I was not there enough, and I am ashamed of the feelings I experienced like anger, that we do not usually associate with grief. But maybe that was just me.

Maybe everyone else is really good at experiencing and acknowledging ambiguous emotions, or maybe I am not alone in feeling the societal pressure - and overt pressure from my family - to be positive and upbeat. Studies have shown, however, that experiencing both positive and negative feelings at the same time can actually promote psychological wellbeing.[24] It has been shown that avoiding the negative feelings can lead to more overeating in individuals who overeat, more relapse in individuals addicted to substances and a decline in people trying to improve their mental health.[25,26]

We live in a society that tells us, "I'll give you something to cry about," "stop crying," "pull yourself up by your bootstraps," and "don't be such a baby!" It tells us not to be so sensitive and dramatic. We also live in a society that says showing emotions, both good and bad, are healthy for us. Is it any wonder we get confused when receiving such conflicting messages? Particularly so if you are a chronic black and white thinker like me.

---

[24] Adler JM, Hershfield HE (2012) Mixed emotional experience is associated with and precedes improvements in psychological well-being. *PLoS ONE* 7(4): e35633. doi:10.1371/journal.pone.0035633

[25] Held, B.S. (2004). The negative side of positive psychology. *Journal of Humanistic Psychology*, Vol. 44, No. 1, pages 9-46.

[26] Kavenagh, D., May J., & Andrade, J. (2009). Tests of the elaborated intrusion theory of craving and desire: Features of alcohol craving during treatment for an alcohol disorder. *British Journal of Clinical Psychology,* 48,(3).

I cannot help but wonder, if part of the reason I was feeling so angry following my dad's death was because I had been suppressing the sadness for so long. If I had to stay happy, I could not possibly feel sad because I had yet to learn that two seemingly contradictory emotions could cooccur. But there is no way to just feel happy about my dad's death, so the next emotion I experienced was anger. Anger is an easy emotion to feel. It allows us to put the blame on someone or something else. It does not require any courage or vulnerability. Where I come from, it is a much more accepted emotion than sadness, which can be perceived as weak.

I was introduced to a Ted Talk© by Brené Brown entitled *The Anatomy of Trust* a few years back.[27] This lady knows her stuff. The first time I was introduced to her was by my boss. She added in there that Brené reminded her of me in a way, with her humor and need to fix things through chronological steps and completion of to-do items. I also think she was telling me, "quit being so stubborn and listen up!" Within minutes of listening to Brené, I knew I had found something that would resonate.

Brené has done several presentations and written several books on her research of courage, vulnerability, empathy, and shame. The concepts that Brené presents are both beautiful and powerful. She has found that embracing shame - that little voice in your head that tells

---

[27] Brown, B. (2010). Anatomy and trust. https://brenebrown.com/videos/anatomy-trust video/, accessed on June 1, 2018.

you that you are not good/strong/pretty enough – and showing up in a vulnerable way, leads to a happier and more fulfilling life. See what was in that sentence there? Vulnerability, shame and happiness. According to Brené, they cannot exist without each other.

I took her advice and jumped in with both feet, committing to make connections with people by admitting my vulnerabilities, like when I was feeling sad and happy and overwhelmed and defeated. Do you know what happened? People showed up for me. I made connections, and I felt more fulfilled. In order to be vulnerable you have to feel vulnerable. And in order to feel vulnerable you must recognize a wide range of emotions including happy, sad, scared, and ashamed.

I cannot lie; I find the words vulnerability and shame to be intimidating. Before I was able to fully embrace what Brené was talking about, I had to try again and again. I would tell my story in the hopes of being vulnerable, but really it was just oversharing disguised as vulnerability. It was sharing for the wrong reasons. It was sharing too much with people who did not deserve to be shared with. Then I would catch it, back it up, and try again. The thing about vulnerability is that you can only be vulnerable if you really know what your truth is. It is being unguarded, but if you do not know what you are guarding, you are not really putting yourself out there.

There are a lot of reasons we do not remember the entirety of an original event. It may be too traumatizing. It may be too humiliating. We may be protecting ourselves. Or it may be the thousands of biases that impact the way we perceive information and experiences.

One of the biases we might experience is the misinformation effect, a cognitive bias that refers to the tendency for post-event information to interfere with the memory of the original event. The misinformation effect illustrates just how easily memories can be influenced and raises concerns about the reliability of memory, particularly in the case of eyewitness memories used to determine criminal guilt.[28]

Am I the only one who has seen this in at least half of the crime shows on television? In addition to its use to provide entertainment in our afternoon television shows, I suspect the misinformation effect also has the ability to alter our memories of people who have died. Since the years my parents have died, discussions with friends and family have had me second guessing my memories of my experiences with my parents, and who they were as people.

Elizabeth Loftus' work on the frailty and fallibility of human memory has explained that, "the misinformation effect refers to the impairment in memory for the past that arises after exposure to misleading information."[28]

This is not to say that stories that have been shared with me were intentionally misleading. I almost wonder if some of the memories were more objective than my own

---

[28] Loftus, E.F. & Hoffman, H.G. (1989). Misinformation and memory: The creation of new memories. *Journal of Experiment Psychology: General, 118: 100-104.*

memories, which were tainted by loss and resentment.

The year after my dad died, some friends and family members developed a trout derby and fundraiser in memory of my dad. I was bitter and angry. My hurt radiated off me like hate for myself and others. Sure, I would participate, but I did not do so in love. I barely participated in any prep work and my offering the day of was to get drunk off cheap, light beer and watch from the sidelines.

By the third year of the trout derby, I started to participate and assist with the organization and planning. During that year, I started to apologize and explain my aversion to the event. It was not the people, the event, or my dad but my own emotions getting in my way. The fifth anniversary of the event came at a time in my life where I was really trying to understand, acknowledge and experience my emotions. I leaned on others and allowed myself to be supported, which to my knowledge was my first experience at doing so. I was real. I was honest in saying that I was overwhelmed by the support, and I acknowledged the tears that were frequently in my eyes throughout that day.

Here's the thing: Those people were there all along. People wanted to be supportive and loving and I simply could not handle it. I do not know if it was shame (what is wrong with needing others?!) or stubbornness, but I am glad I let it go. The day of that event was emotional. It was happy and sad. I admitted to being anxious. It was beautiful. In allowing myself to experience a range of emotions, I did not one time feel mad. It may have been the first time in five years that I don't recall the red anger monster lurking right around the corner.

During the research and development of this book -that is the fancy term for trying to figure out how to put all these damn ideas on paper - I originally wrote: "What do conflicting emotions do to your mental health?" When reading that note, I interpreted it as, "what damage is it doing?" Upon reading it again, I think what the conflicting emotions really do is build us. It makes us who we are. It allows us to live. If we do not feel the bad stuff, we would not know how good the good stuff is.

To help ourselves not get swept away in the sea of emotions, we can practice mindfulness. That is such a dainty and pretty word for the amount of work it takes. Maybe it does not have to be a lot of work, but I certainly make it that way. The times I have found it most helpful is when I am experiencing heavy emotions like anger and sadness and I just admit it. I will say to myself or someone I trust, "I am just feeling really sad today," and then I will just give myself time to feel it. Okay, so this has only happened a dozen times because I am just learning and still a work in progress. I can certainly attest to the fact that it has helped me to accept the emotions and work through them.

This whole mindfulness thing seems like a hella cool way to feel the feels and keep myself mentally healthy. By taking each moment as it is, with honesty and vulnerability, I am on my way to just that.

Empathy and Apathy

As a social worker, the word empathy is thrown around like confetti. We are introduced to it in textbooks and through experience. Likely, the experiences we have encountered before we even enter formal schooling is what led us to the career in the first place. I would also suggest that it is something we develop before we are able to label it.

I have had the ability to connect with people from a young age. I remember feeling empathetic and encouraging of classmates in elementary school who were being bullied. I remember feeling as though others trusted me at a young age. Taking others' perspectives and trying to enter conversations judgment-free is something I continue to practice today.

When I was in third grade, I asked my mom, "why are people so mean?" She responded with a phrase I remind myself of on a daily, if not weekly basis: "People are mean because they're hurting on the inside." Over the years, I have started to understand what this means on a much deeper level. It was a great way to start to understand empathy and perspective-taking. It helped me to take a step back and consider where someone's pain is coming from. It helps to understand that more often than not, someone's hurtful behavior is not about me. Ultimately, it allows me to empathize with them.

Conversely, despite my ability to view things from others' points of view, it was not until recent years that I started to connect empathizing with someone to giving them the benefit of the doubt. Do not misread this. I am not saying they are the same things. What I am proposing is that giving the benefit of the doubt to someone is much easier if you are being empathetic towards that person.

During the first few months of exploring the practice of giving the benefit of the doubt, or "BOD treatment" as I like to call it, I had a conversation with a colleague. We were discussing a difficult situation in which I was being challenged to problem-solve. I do not recall what solution I came up with, but I do remember him saying, "Brenna, who benefits from giving the benefit of the doubt? We do not do it for other people, you know."

This was a revolutionary idea for me. What do you mean we do not do it for other people? Thinking that people have the best intentions is certainly a benefit to them as well as us. The reason I have fought tooth and nail to not give the benefit of the doubt was for fear of being taken advantage of and not fully trusting other people. I understand his point. It is liberating not to be thinking the worst of people all the time. There is a sense of peace when we try to empathize with, take the perspective of, and then assume the best of the person we may be battling. This, if approached with a sense of earnestness, brings us peace. In the words of Wonder Woman, "only love can truly save the world."

This idea was brought together for me through the works, *Leadership and Self-Deception, Anatomy of Being,* and *Way of Being.*[29,30,31] The books propose similar ideas and give concrete examples on how to treat others as you wish to be treated.

I was introduced to the book *Leadership and Self-Deception* by a peer of mine. It presents its ideas in the form of a story, so it is easy to read and relatively easy to understand - beyond the whole "blowing my mind" thing. Within the first few pages, it presents an incredibly flattering (read: totally unflattering) idea that if others around you are not performing how you want them to, they are not the problem, you are. The idea is when we believe others are the problem, we are experiencing self-deception or being in the box. Being in the box prevents us from seeing other people as people. We want to see other people as people. That means that

---

[29] Arbinger Institute (2016). The outward mindset: Seeing beyond ourselves. San Francisco, CA: Berrett-Koehler Publishers.

[30] Arbinger Institute (2006). The anatomy of peace. San Francisco, CA: Berrett-Koehler Publishers.

[31] Arbinger Institute (2010). Leadership and self-deception: Getting out of the box. San Francisco, CA: Berrett-Koehler Publishers.

we are considering their wants and needs as people, rather than as objects to help us get what we want and need. When we see other people as people, they are able to return the favor of viewing us as people and therefore consider our wants and needs.

If you are into operationalizing everything you read into simple steps and rules like I am, then you will love this next part. The work of the Arbinger Institute explores how:

1. People in conflict all wait for the other party to change. Therefore, conflicts linger.
2. If you are going to invite change in others, there is something that must first change in you.
3. If you want others to agree with you, then you care about how they view you, and you need them to see you as a person. For this reason, you need to see them as a person first.
4. If someone really is "bad" or "wrong," we can still hold ourselves to the same standard we are demanding of them.
5. I become an agent of change only to the degree that I begin to live to help things go right, rather than simply to correct things that are wrong.

There are sometimes at which it makes more sense to be who you are and if someone does not like it, then heck 'em. Unfortunately, I have not found this to be a productive way to build meaningful relationships or advance my career.

We seem to be raised in this split world, where we are either not supposed to care what other people think or we are supposed to allow people to walk all over us. *Leadership and Self-Deception* certainly seems to be encouraging its readers to be a bunch of big softies in the first few pages. Upon further exploration, it proposes that if you want to get what you need out of relationships, you have to extend respect and consideration for others in order to receive the same respect and consideration in return. You can maintain your boundaries and self-respect and still find a way to extend the benefit of the doubt.

Even though *Leadership and Self-Deception* was all about leadership and management in the workplace, the concepts were easily generalized to my personal life. I started explaining it to my husband and my close friends; I gave a presentation to the team I supervise. I was committed to sharing this information with everyone, because it was the best playbook I had ever seen on how to live the golden rule of "treat others as you wish to be treated."

In full disclosure, when I started exploring this work and these concepts, I was overwhelmed. It was unflattering to the ways that I have thought and experienced life for many years. Essentially, they propose that our way of being towards someone - how we are truly seeing them, judging them, what we are believing about them - surpasses what we are doing or saying. This relates deeply to our emotions, in the sense that if we do not admit our negative emotions, we will continue to pretend we are positive and happy without feeling that way. Thus, we will invite others to fake ways of being positive and miss out on connections and true happiness.

I read all three of the Arbinger Institute books because that is what I do: I hear about a new concept, obsess about it, learn as much as I can about it, then make it my new life goal. Many things in my life that I have obsessed about are quite productive things, and this was one of them. Out-of-the-box thinking is taking the perspective of someone else to consider what wants and needs are driving their actions. This theory promotes great leadership, which will help to form productive teams. It is also a great way to conceptualize empathy.

I could not put a number on the times I have experienced empathy, on the giving or receiving end. More times than I can count, people have said to me, “I have no idea how you do it.” With watching my dad become ill and wither away over 10 years and losing both my parents at a young age, I have heard the phrase a lot. I get it. It is a strange scenario, and I am in a small town. I am grateful that my parents were kind and generous people because it left me and my siblings a safety net to fall into after they passed. I think it left a lot of people at a loss for words. Even after years since my dad’s diagnosis and the loss of my parents, people still say that to me when I share my story.

My response for years has been, “we each know our own worst pain.” I do not know if I heard that somewhere or if it developed as the best-received response over the years, but I believe it to my core. Sometimes the conversations go on further in which I explain that they would survive through it just like I did because we all do what we have to do. Whether someone dies slowly from cancer or quickly in a car accident, they are still dead, leaving others grieving in their wake. There is no point to compare our situations when pain is not finite. There is enough pain and kindness in the world to empathize, rather than compete with one another over who has it worse.

A month or two after my mom died, I was talking on the phone with a dear friend from college. She shared that her mom had gone to inpatient rehabilitation for detox from alcoholism. I remember her saying she did not want to put it on me with all I had going on. Perhaps this was the first time I said we all know our own worst pain. I remember my heart hurting for her. Hurting because I felt like, "what was I if I could not be there for her when she needed support too?" Hurting because she was hurting and not feeling like she could reach out to me because of my experiences.

On more than one occasion I have had conversations about how I also like to be there for my friends, and as such, I need them to trust me with their pain, even if they think I cannot handle it. Perhaps as I learn boundaries and learn to say when I cannot handle what they are dealing with, I will become more trustworthy because they know I will tell them if I am feeling overloaded.

I am not sure if that is evidence of my ability to empathize with others, or a show of my preference to run instead of confronting my feelings. If I focus on what someone else is going through, I do not have to acknowledge my own feelings and experiences. Caring about others' needs to avoid our own feelings should not be confused with empathy. It is not a flattering thought, but it is a defense mechanism that I have practiced over the years. Part of my upbringing – in which I received confusing messages about how to acknowledge, or not acknowledge, my feelings – led to some tactics on how to divert my attention from what I am feeling. I control, I plan, I perform, I clean, I exercise, I help others. Basically, I do anything and everything to avoid feeling. This shouldn't be confused with apathy. Apathy is disinterest, lack of concern, or dispassion. I believe my feelings were so strong that I could not handle them.

Sometimes, people will share that they see me as the strongest person who handled my grief with grace. This seems shocking to me as many days I truly felt like I was just surviving. If I think of resilience as my ability to overcome adversity and continue my normal development, I know that any resilience I have shown is an absolute testament to the notion that social support and connections build resilience.[32,33]

My mom was an amazing woman. She had her flaws, as we all do, but she was a top-notch mom. Part of grieving

---

[32] *Resilience Research Institute* (2018). Resilience. Retrieved July 17, 2018 from http://www.resilienceproject.org/about-the-rrc/resilience.

[33] U.S. Department of Veterans Affairs (2018). PTSD: National Centers for PTSD. Retrieved from https://www.ptsd.va.gov/family/effect_relationships.asp

the loss of someone is not to demonize or put them on a pedestal so I say this with good balance. My mom told me all the time that I did not come with a manual, but for the most part her instincts were on point. I believe the parenting that I received from my mom particularly, is responsible for my ability to remain strong despite adversity. She was an amazing role model in many ways – as a mother and as a kind person.

It comes as no surprise that it has been shown that parents who exhibit high empathy are better able to understand and to respond to their children's changing needs. My mother's way of being allowed for a warm and nurturing relationship. This type of parenting has been shown to be negatively associated with antisocial behaviors – meaning the more nurturing and warmth, the less antisocial behaviors.[34] mom, a woman who cultivated such a caring and loving relationship with me, was the same woman who showed great empathy by teaching me that people say and do hurtful things because they are hurting on the inside. I feel lucky to have learned such a valuable lesson, because it has allowed me to put that love and kindness out in the world and receive it back in many ways during the challenging times in my life.

I need to be clear here, that I know my experiences could be far worse. There will always be someone better and

---

[34] Crocetti, E., et al (2016). The dynamic interplay among maternal Empathy, Quality of Mother-Adolescent Relationship, and Adolescent Antisocial Behaviors: New Insights from a Six-Wave Longitudinal Multi-Informant Study. *PLoS One, 11*(3). doi: 10.1371/journal.ponc.0150009

worse off than you, and my situation is no different. I was loved, hugged and provided for growing up. I did not want for much. I grew up in a white, middle-ish- class family. My need to justify myself – to explain my story – speaks exactly to what I am talking about with the comparison between each of our experiences.

Perhaps what we as a society need to be focusing on is not what sets us all apart but what can bring us together. What would the world look like if we were empathetic and attempted to understand one another – whether we are privileged or not, grieving or not, worse or better off?

Studies have shown that feeling empathy towards others is associated with acceptance of other people, even if they are a member of another group (i.e., different race, gender, socioeconomic status).[31] It has also been shown that we experience more positive feelings for individuals when we empathize with them, and we feel more empathetic to the group that we associate them with (i.e., all people of that specific socioeconomic status, race, etc.).[35]

Empathy has played such an important role in my life, both personally and professionally. Being empathic is what allows us to connect with other humans, to show love and understanding. I had my first date with my husband in 2011. My mom had died two years prior, I was completing my final semester of my undergraduate

---

[35] Wheeler, H. & Quinn, C. (2017) Can Facebook aid sustainability? An investigation of empathy expression within the humans of New York Blog. *Sustainability* 9(6).

degree, and I was starting to feel secure with no having a boyfriend for the first time that I could remember. On our first date, I was impressed by his button-up shirt and fancy shoes and that he made me laugh. He turned up "booty poppin'" music on the way to dinner and we danced and laughed during the drive. When we got to the restaurant, our conversation drifted to our life stories. We shared recent experiences which had left us in transition, and talked about our grieving periods. I explained my mom died in 2009 and he shared that his mother was involved in a violent crime that landed her in prison for 6-15 years during the same year. We cried together as we connected over the trauma and the shared feelings of being motherless. We empathized with one another and it allowed us to connect in a way we likely would not have without our recent experiences.

The term empathy dates back to literature from the 1800s. It is referenced frequently in self-help books, quality-of-care discussions for medical health, and rapport-building and therapeutic techniques in mental health treatment. I have found the most easily understood definition of empathy to be: The ability to feel or imagine another person's emotional experience.

Intellectualizing things is a hobby of mine. While it is fun to define empathy, I also find it enjoyable to explore reasons why we do things. Before I took the path of social work, I wanted to be a psychologist. In fact, my undergraduate degree is in psychology. I struggled through some of my psychology classes – neuropsychology and psychopharmacology (barf). But I also found some pieces of psychology to be helpful, in understanding why we are the way we are and to provide some insight on why we do the things we do.

If you have been reading this book - rather than just skimming the pages because you bought it out of respect for me or were gifted it by that family member that could not figure out what to get you - you read about cognitive biases earlier, when I was talking about black-and-white thinking. Cognitive biases and the like get me going right in the nerd feels. There are a few biases that prevent us from connecting and inhibit our ability to feel empathetic. The fundamental attribution error is the tendency for us to place blame on an internal cause of someone else rather than an external factor. Conversely, the actor-Observer bias is the tendency for us to attribute the problems of our own faults on external factors, rather than internal.[36]

For example, you are on your way to work and are driving a few miles an hour faster than the speed limit, because you do not want to be late for your first meeting of the day. You come upon a driver going 5 mph under the speed limit and pass them while staring them down out the passenger window. You are late for goodness' sake, this is not a time for slowpokes and why is that idiot going so slow? A mile down the road, a car comes up on your tailgate so close you cannot see their front bumper in your rearview mirror. In the next passing

---

[36] Jones, E. & Nisbett, R. (1971). The actor and the observer: Divergent perceptions of the causes of behavior. New York, NY: General Learning Press.

lane, they zip pass you and are staring you down out their passenger window. How dare they? They are such an irresponsible driver! Rather than seeing the potential of the first driver having a fear of going fast or concern for a child in the back, we assume it is their nature. We are more likely to assume that our own behavior can be blamed on the slow poke and that others' behavior is blamed on the fact they are an asshole. The layman's term for this might be hypocrisy or double standards.

The fundamental attribution error is a total barrier to our ability to be empathetic. It is essential to look at situations, and the people involved in them, non-judgmentally.

I have struggled for a long time with trust and empathy. I have never really understood why I would want to give people the benefit of the doubt - would that not just provide them the opportunity to screw me over? As with everything else you have read and will read, there is a reason you and I are the way we are. Maybe I have been burned by someone to whom I tried to give the benefit of the doubt then generalized that experience to all relationships because you know, that is what I do - create rules and all.

When my colleague that day asked me for whom we give the benefit of the doubt, it was not until he asked that question that I realized the answer: Me. I am the one who benefits when giving the benefit of the doubt. I have learned over time that sometimes people do not deserve that treatment because they have burned me in the past. If I keep giving the benefit of the doubt regardless, I can sleep easier at night. I can feel peace because I can think about how and why they might have done what they did (i.e., what need or want were they trying to fulfill). It does not mean I have to trust them again, but I can empathize with them from a distance. We empathize for our own benefit when it would be easy to distrust all in order to protect ourselves. If we want to avoid the paradox of either/or, we need to take each moment we are presented with and use our best judgement on whether or not we are going to give the benefit of the doubt, whether or not we are going to empathize, and keep in mind that ultimately, we are the ones who benefit.

Forgiveness and Revenge

When I was about 14, I was sitting in the back seat of the family car with my brother and sister, driving on some family vacation. My brother and I were picking on each other and somehow his fist flung loose and punched me in the eye. I do not remember how badly it hurt, but am assuming I whined and cried like my children do now when their sibling hurts them in some way. My dad pulled the car over, pulled my brother and me out of the back seat, held my brother's arms behind his back and told me to hit him in the face and make it even. I do not recall for a second wanting to hit him back. Sure I was mad, but I knew he had not done it on purposc and I had no desire to get even. Frankly, even if he had done it on purpose, hurting someone just to hurt them is not really my style.

This experience was consistent with my dad often

saying, “an eye for an eye.” I remember him saying if somebody hits you, you hit them back. Ironically, the saying of an eye for an eye as referenced in the Christian Bible is describing the prohibition of such behavior, encouraging Christians to turn the other cheek instead. My dad was baptized a Christian and was not nearly as open-minded as me. I am certain he would have balked if I had the opportunity to explain to him that the religious proclamations associated with such behavior was in the Quran as ordained for the children of Islam, and in the Torah for people who practice Judaism. Regardless, to some extent I see his point. Perhaps that is me embracing the gray, because while I see his perspective, I tend to prefer the practice of, “two wrongs don’t make a right,” which is more consistent with Bible-based teachings.

I suppose both make sense in some ways. If a stranger attacks me on the street, you better believe I am going to scratch, kick, hit, and claw back. If my kid starts getting bullied and someone tries to hit him, I am going to suggest that my kid hit back if there are not any other solutions. An important piece to consider is: What other solutions are available? Did my son try to remove himself from the situation? Did he tell a teacher, an adult, me or my husband? Did he ask the other kid to stop? If other options have been exhausted and my kid is still in danger, you bet I support him hitting back. Just like I support your kid to hit mine back if it gets to that point. I also support your daughter kicking my kid in the balls if he crosses the line after being told no. My greatest goal in life is to see to it that my child never puts your child in those positions, so fingers crossed I never have to tell him, "sorry kid, but you had that coming."

I cannot support acting in a vicious, malicious, or violent way just because somebody else did. You are entitled to your beliefs, religion-based or otherwise, but you are not entitled to act on beliefs that might harm another person. Because I take the approach of understanding others' mean acts as a way in which they might be expressing pain, I find the whole "eye for an eye" thing to be counterproductive. They hurt me, I hurt them, so they are hurt and hurt me back, and on and on. Sometimes we have to take a step back and identify what our win is really going to look like. If your goal is to hurt as many people as you can, then sure, revenge is a great thing.

Likely, and hopefully, that is not your goal. Think of it in terms of beliefs inequality. If the beliefs of a feminist were to include man-hating by definition, it would perpetuate a culture of inequality. By definition, to have a feminist point of view is to seek equality, not to be better than. If we end up with inequality at the expense of others, we have failed to meet our overall goal.

Similarly, if someone makes a mistake, engaging in an act of violence or aggression in order to hurt them is not going to solve anything. It is not going to reduce their hurt nor reduce future chances of them perpetrating hurt again.

It is not realistic to expect humans not to hurt one

another. We are human, and we do make mistakes. As humans we have a long history of making mistakes and hurting others, as evidenced by the creation of the word forgiveness many years back. Forgiveness is represented in the Bible thousands of years ago, but it is not a religious word at its core. In old English it is translated as "to give up desire or power to punish.[37]

When defined that way, the act and idea of forgiveness is quite beautiful. As with many things, it is easier said than done. I understand that if I hurt someone, it may be difficult to forgive me. This is particularly true when my intentions are brought to light. If I had the best of intentions anyway, the best I can do is communicate those intentions and ask for forgiveness. The easiest way to make this connection is to focus on accountability.

If I do something that unintentionally hurts your feelings, the best I can do is own it; "I am so sorry that my behavior impacted you like that, as it was not my intention." I might even further explain my circumstances and what else may have contributed to my behavior, such as an argument with my husband, the loss of a loved one or my recent symptoms of depression. Sharing these things is not for the sake of making excuses. When we take accountability, we open the door to connection and vulnerability. When we do that, those we have hurt can see us as a person, rather than as a threat to their safety.

---

[37] English Language & Usage (2019). Etymology of the word "forgive". Retrieved from https://english.stackexchange.com/questions/343990/etymology-of-word-forgive

Accountability is one of my strongest values. I strive to display it, and I look for it in others. If someone else can apologize for their behavior and show insight in to how it impacted someone else, they are easier to forgive. I know I am not the first to believe it, but whenever we talk about forgiveness, it is important to remember that forgiveness does not mean forgetting. We can forgive someone, release our desires to get even with someone, but still consider their behavior as a predictor of future behaviors. We can use the information to set boundaries and judge future circumstances.

Some may describe forgiveness as weak, but I challenge you to consider who forgiveness is for. Frankly, the person forgiven does not even need to know. It is not about them anyway. It is about deciding to no longer give power to the person who hurt us. When we forgive, we take back our power to control our own energy and we determine to no longer waste it on someone who caused us pain.

It is interesting to think that it took so long for me to understand why we give others the benefit of the doubt considering I had gained an understanding of forgiveness nearly a decade ago. Some of it was certainly religiously based. There are so many gospels on forgiving others as Jesus has done for us, but it also went beyond that for me. I do not recall the story of the instance it happened, but I do know I had a realization of, "holy crap. Do you know who benefits from forgiving that person? Me. I am the one who finds peace."

It is argued that forgiveness is the key to happiness.[38] One study found that those who practiced forgiveness had less anger, less stress, less rumination, and lowered reactivity in comparison to those who held onto their anger and pain.[39]

Because of the impact that forgiving a wrongdoing can have, it is imperative that we know how to go about forgiving. Remember when I said earlier that forgiving is easier said than done? The practice of that is true, but people have been studying how to accomplish forgiveness for years.

Everett Worthington identified the following five steps - called REACH - in order to achieve forgiveness:

1. Recall the hurt
2. Empathize with the one who hurt you
3. Altruistic gift of forgiveness
4. Commit to forgive
5. Hold on to the forgiveness[40]

It is argued that true altruism, or selfless concern for the

---

[38] Positive Psychology. (2019). Forgiveness: The key to a happier future. Retrieved from https://positivepsychology.com/forgiveness/

[39] Harris, A. H., et al. (2001). Effects of group forgiveness intervention on perceived stress, state and trait, anger, symptoms of stress, self-reported health and forgiveness. *Journal of Clinical Psychology*, 62 (6), 715-733

[40] Worthington, E. (2019). REACH forgiveness. Retrieved from http://www.evworthington-forgiveness.com/reach-forgiveness/

benefit of others, is unattainable. Even if we try to do something for a seemingly altruistic reason, we also benefit because of the satisfaction of helping someone else. If you are able to practice forgiveness simply for the benefit of the other person, good for you. I have found that is just not something that works for me. I spent many years trying to be perfect and consider others' needs at the sacrifice to my own wellbeing. While it might sound jaded or bitter, I now wonder if, "I do not take care of myself, who will?" Some might say they rely on God or a higher power to protect them, but that was not something that worked for me either.

Without the altruistic aspect – Worthington's step 3 – I could see that step being changed from altruism to account. Once you empathize with the one who hurt you, account for your own peace and happiness that would result from your forgiving the act of wrong doing.

If forgiveness impacts our happiness, how does it interact with anger or aggression? When I was in my second year of college – the year before my mother died, the year I reclaimed my virginity during a time of compulsive church-attending behavior – I attended a mixed martial arts class in the inner-city of Grand Rapids, Michigan. I went twice per week with a friend of mine, and we would train for three hours each night. We started with 100 pushups and 100 sit-ups. I got strong during this time, and learned how to kick, punch, knee, and elbow another person effectively. Another thing I noticed during that time though, was how aggressive I felt – even when I was not at a training session.

I have always been a bit spicy, and definitely more so since the death of my mother and dad. That time in my life was not one that I would associate with emotional turmoil causing my anger. Rather, I associate my increased aggressive behavior with my participation in kickbox training. Studies have shown an association between violent video games, as well as being spanked as a child, with future engagement in violent behaviors.[41,42] Studies have also found that individuals who have forgiven crimes experience less aggression.[43] All of this leads one to believe that aggression and peace truly are related. Whether you do so altruistically or selfishly, taking the opportunity to let go of the need for revenge when someone has hurt you is way to experience happiness.

---

[41] Association for Psychological Science. (2017). Spanking linked to increase in children's behavior problems. Retrieved from https://www.psychologicalscience.org/news/releases/spanking-linked-to-increase-in-childrens-behavior-problems.html

[42] Goldbeck, L. & Pew, A. (2019). Violent video games and aggression. *National Center for Health Research*. Retrieved from http://www.center4research.org/violent-video-games-can-increase-aggression/

[43] Webb, J.R., Dula, C.S., & Brewer, K. (2012). Forgiveness and aggression among college students. *Journal of Spirituality in Mental Health*, 14(1):38-58

Selfish and Self-Care

Listen. I am not claiming to know what I am doing with my life here. More often than not, I question what the hell I am doing; how to parent; how to stay healthy; how to make a professional legacy; how to stay sane. You name it, I have questioned it. One thing I have learned through loss and grief is the importance of self-care. For me, this looks like a lot of different things. When I was first starting my career, I would go out on the weekends and sing karaoke. Alcohol involved or not, I love getting on stage and singing.

My mom tried to start teaching me the importance of self-care at a young age. She would set up little spas in her master bath with a bean bag, nail polish and foot baths. She showed me how to push back and trim my cuticles, file my nails, massage my feet, neck, and shoulders. She tried to teach me the importance of caring for myself physically, presumably so I would know how to care for myself emotionally. I have learned many phrases - mantras if you will - over the years to remind myself about self-care. "You can't pour from an empty cup" is probably one of my favorites. Basically, we want to fill our own cup before we fill those of others. It is simple, really. If I want to save the life of someone else, I have first to save myself.

If you are on a plane and the oxygen masks drop, and you decide to put it on someone else before yourself, you risk passing out from lack of oxygen, rather than completing the assistance to someone else. You would be no help to others if you pass out.

I like to think of myself as a giver. Maybe that is being a martyr. I think if you asked someone how they would describe me, they would say I am a great listener. I hear it all the time: "You are so easy to talk to." That is a wonderful thing. It is reaffirming that I went into social work when people tell me or behave in a way that says they trust me. Some of this comes from people-pleasing, from the desire to be perfect, to be well-liked, or to make the other person happy.

It is also beneficial to me though, because it allows me to run from my own feelings and emotions. When someone else is sharing their story and feelings with me, it takes the attention off of me. Sometimes, this is not so good. If you are constantly asking about others and meeting others' needs, you fail to ask for what you need. If you fail to ask for what you need, it is likely you are not going to get the support in the way you need. And then your needs are going to be unmet. When my needs are unmet, I am cranky. The need might be hunger, fatigue, quiet, love or hugs. It might be a shoulder to cry on, or an ear to listen. If you do not ask the people in your life for what you need, you are not giving them a fair shot. I have also heard relationships compared to finance, which is interesting for a lot of reasons. I have always been impulsive. I learned at a young age the joy you could experience from buying things - from obtaining and getting things. We had a string of multiple funerals in my family and each time we would say, “retail therapy” and buy ourselves something new. It is not surprising, then, that I can be a bit impulsive with relationships, with boundaries, and with my heart.

My dad tried to teach me about investing. I know the basics: If you want to make money, you have to spend/invest it. You do not want to invest your money just anywhere; you want to invest it somewhere where you will get the greatest returns. In the same way, you want to be in relationships where the more you give, the more you get. If you have asked and they fail to give you what you need, time and time again, they may not be worth the investment.

Similarly, you cannot make a payment from an empty bank account. If you did not have any money in your bank account, would you be going around passing out $20 bills to everyone? If you are failing to take care of yourself, you cannot pass out the encouragement and love coins to others.

Self-care can look like a lot of different things depending on who you are, what you enjoy, and what makes you happy. It also depends on the day. Somedays, self-care to me looks like a hot shower and then a fan that keeps my face cool while I spend quiet, uninterrupted time to blow dry my hair. Some days, it is a manicure and pedicure at a salon where I do not know a soul; where I can sit in silence and not talk to anyone except to say, "this color; rounded straight; thank you." Sometimes it is a 45-minute workout where I can listen to the boom of my music and zone out into what my body can do. I am learning what makes me feel good and when I am seriously lacking in self-care. If I do not take time for it, I hurt both myself and others.

I think of the times when I first became a parent, when my husband and I navigated our suddenly much-reduced playtime to meet our self-care needs. He was much better at it than I, going to visit friends or spending time out working on his boat to refuel his emotional tank. I felt like if I was not doing something for my child, husband, family or job that I was wasting time.

Since having a second child, and a significant amount of therapy, I have learned to better advocate for what I need. It might be yoga; it might be alone time; it might be watching a show I enjoy. If I do not advocate for that, I tend to go in one of two directions: I either ride on the high for a while, looking at those around me as if they are beneath me because they are not doing it all; or I become burned out, sinking into depression and blaming everyone around me for having to do it all. I get grumpy and frankly, a little mean. I get so tired from "doing it all," that I might not do anything. When I take care of myself and ask for what I need, I feel more confident, even if I am doing a little less. I am kind and generous to myself and to others around me, because I can recognize that we are all doing the best we can with what we have. The preventative measure of asking for a night away when I feel myself slipping is worth far more than letting myself slide into a world of self-pity and monster-like bitchiness.

Have you ever been in a conversation with someone and you feel the need to solve their problems and give advice? Or maybe you have been on the talking end when really what you need is someone to listen, and the so-called listener will not stop talking long enough to let you get your story out. My mom used to remind me frequently of a time that I came home talking about my day, and she tried suggesting idea after idea to solve the problem until I just huffed, "I just need to vent!" She reminded herself of that out loud several times over the years, and I was able to get my needs met. I am not saying we should yell things like that at our partners, friends or family, but there is definitely a way to say, "I just had a really hard day, and I do not need you to try to fix it but I do need you to just listen."

Sometimes self-care is applying the brakes to people-pleasing. One of the things I learned from the Arbinger Institute is that thinking about someone else's needs does not mean that you automatically have to meet those needs. Approaching conversations and relationships from that out-of-the-box thinking is simply saying that you have thought and considered their perspective. For many years I thought that in order to be a kind and generous person, I had to give and give and give to meet other people's needs. With this new information I am able to hear a friend's request, consider their needs and my needs, and speak genuinely about whether or not I have the capacity to help them.

Reducing people-pleasing is so much about creating boundaries and recognizing that you simply cannot do or give everything for everyone all the time without sacrificing your own wellbeing. Some might argue that if we had a world full of people-pleasers there would be less violence, more generosity, and more equality. The thing about people-pleasing, though, is that it can lead to bitterness and resentment. When I am feeling resentful, I act passive-aggressive and spiteful. Those things together do not lead to peace. And who is to say that the people we are trying to please all have the same motives and goals? What if I was trying to please Hitler? I say that slightly tongue-in-cheek, but in the scenarios of a world full of people-pleasers, we would likely continue to hate, and engage in war and violence.

The armor I have equipped myself with – against a lifelong people-pleasing session – is boundaries. We have opportunities every day to set both big and small boundaries. There are many factors that contribute to how we might accomplish boundary setting. One factor is who the boundary is with. It is much more difficult to tell someone you are close with that you cannot spend time with them anymore, because their negativity creates a toxic relationship. At the same time, it can be much easier to use small opportunities over time to say what you are and are not comfortable with. I had to learn that boundary setting starts when you ask for something you need. For example, if someone says something that offends you and you tell them that you would appreciate it that they did not speak that way around you, you are setting a boundary by asking for what you need to feel comfortable. If they respect it, your relationship is strengthened. If they do not, it feels less safe. It leads to another situation in which you have to set a larger boundary. Next time they say the same thing that offends you, you might have to say, "Come on, man, I told you before that really bothers me. I don't really want to hang out when you talk like that."

Setting boundaries and doing things for others because we want to, not just because we want to please others, is a form of self-care. If we prioritize ourselves in a healthy way like this, helping others can be done in a kind and generous way. Think of a situation you have been in when you have been invited to two different events. One might be a retirement party for a close colleague at work and the other might be a dinner with a friend from out of town. Simply having the thought of how much it might mean to those people for you to be present, is generous in itself. When you think that way, you can then explain with kindness how you would love to participate in both, but you simply cannot be in two places at once. Now, you could try to spend a short amount of time at both, thinking the whole time about how it is impacting both close friends and then rushing to drive a half an hour in between so you can get to both. That kind of decision is certainly people-pleasing - and for me it is downright exhausting. Nobody is getting the best of me and it is not a way I can take care of myself.

Knowing I am a relatively green social worker, and in addition to what I learned from my mom, I see an ongoing movement happening emphasizing the importance of self-care. People may have been suggesting and begging for this for years but for me it feels new.

At my current place of employment, we are reminded of the importance of self-care frequently. Working at a community mental health agency with populations in which the majority, if not everyone, have experienced trauma puts our staff at high risk of secondary trauma. Secondary trauma occurs when someone is exposed to people who have been traumatized themselves, disturbing descriptions of traumatic events by a survivor, or others inflicting cruelty on one another.[44] Because of our high risk, our leadership emphasizes the importance of self-care in an effort to reduce the impact of the secondary trauma we experience. I have been lucky to receive many trainings on how to care for myself whether it be through exercise, meditation, yoga, drinking more water, seeing a therapist, dancing, singing or taking time off to be with family.

Some people see the times in which you are advocating for self-care and boundaries as selfish. The summer my

---

[44] Secondary Trauma (2010). Secondary trauma. Retrieved from http://www.secondarytrauma.org/

mom died, I took off to Brooklyn, New York, with my aunt and her family. I am sure one of the reasons I did this was to escape the house we lived in and the reminders in every corner of the woman I had just lost. But when I reflect back, I also think of how self-loving that was. I decided not to spend the summer working six days a week to save money for an upcoming college semester I likely would not attend, because I would stay home with my ill father and younger brother instead, as we transitioned to a new life without our wife/mom. Instead, I spent my summer taking yoga and spin classes and journaling at local coffee shops. I spent evenings with my cousins playing games or exploring the city. I can recall two calls from family and friends back home, who expressed their dissatisfaction with my decision. One went as far as to tell me how my behavior was selfish and self-sabotaging.

I have come to learn that people who see self-care as selfish have yet to learn the importance of boundaries and self-care themselves. Perhaps if we all focus more on taking care of ourselves, there would be more room for love, generosity, and kindness in the moments that we support others.

Sickness and Health

We hear the word health every time we turn a corner, and how it is described is constantly changing. I have a history of taking everything to an extreme, so a compulsive need to be healthy can turn into something unhealthy. I have said for many years, "I just want to be healthy." It is such a strange desire because it leads to a question that changes depending on who you are talking to: What is health?

As a social worker, I know that health is not just inclusive of our physical health. When my dad was diagnosed with ALS, I watched him and my mom talk about how he was going to "fight" the disease. I watched my gruff, hardworking father - who I had never heard even utter the word "organic" before - switch our household to all organic foods, organic toothpaste and organic deodorant. I remember him having his metal fillings replaced with white porcelain fillings. He picked up yoga. Yoga! He practiced saying "I love you." I watched a man whose physical health was failing, with sickness and disease taking over his nerves and muscles, start to embody different meanings of the word health.

When I think about it now, it was certainly a time in my life when I started to learn a lot about wellness, homeopathic treatments, and the various parts to health beyond what we can see from an outsider's perspective. When you looked at my dad in those beginning years, you could not tell he was sick. There are many diseases that attack their victims' bodies in ways that we cannot see with the naked eye. Sure, our medical world has developed to the point of identifying genes, bacteria, viruses and other workings of the body to be able to quantify numbers and symptoms of what is considered healthy and what is considered ill. However, if health was as simple as physical workings of the body, we would have a treatment or cure for everything. This is likely a thought other individual have had as well, when they started looking into other factors affecting physical health.

Consider the Centers for Disease Control and Prevention (CDC) and Kaiser Permanente Adverse Childhood Effects (ACEs) study that looked at how specific incidents of trauma, abuse, and neglect in childhood - sexual abuse, verbal abuse, a parent who was incarcerated, a parent who was mentally ill or had a substance abuse issue – were correlated with studied adults' physical health status and behaviors.[45] The study was developed when a doctor noted a high prevalence of individuals who were obese and also reported a history of sexual abuse or violence. The participants of the study were close to 50% male and 50% female, primarily Caucasian (74.8%), with at least some college (75.2%).

This study found that ACEs are common – 2/3 of the participants had at least one, and more than 1 in 5 reported 3 or more ACEs. The CDC reports that the more ACEs an individual reports, the higher the risk the individual has for the following:

Alcoholism and alcohol abuse

Chronic obstructive pulmonary disease

Depression

Fetal death

Health-related quality of life

Illicit drug use

Ischemic heart disease

Liver disease

Poor work performance

Financial stress

Risk for intimate partner violence

Multiple sexual partners

Sexually transmitted diseases

Smoking

Suicide attempts

Unintended pregnancies

---

[45] Center for Disease Control and Prevention (2019). About the CDC-Kaiser ACE Study. Retrieved from https://www.cdc.gov/violenceprevention/childabuseandneglect/acestudy/about.html?CDC_AA_refVal=https%3A%2F%2Fwww.cdc.gov%2Fviolenceprevention%2Facestudy%2Fabout.html

Early initiation of smoking

Early initiation of sexual activity

Adolescent pregnancy

Risk for sexual violence

Poor academic achievement

I remember being trained on this for the first time and thinking: "Oh great, that's just great, now what? Are we all doomed?" It felt discouraging. Here we have found an important link between the negative impact of experiences such as abuse, neglect, parents who are mentally ill, incarcerated or divorced - and the increased risk it creates for mental and physical illness. The ACEs study is frequently presented to discuss the importance of intervening and attempting to reduce abuse and neglect.

We cannot possibly intervene into every child's life to prevent these adverse experiences from happening. Not to mention, um hello, some of us are beyond our childhood years and what does that mean for us? It is powerful information. Yes, we should intervene. Yes, it teaches us about certain reasons we may be the way we are, that go beyond what we eat or how much exercise we get.

Something else I learned that had me sighing in relief is how we can build resilience and reduce the impacts of ACEs. Resilience is built through basic needs being met, social support and community, and knowledge of parent and child development.[46] It is fascinating stuff. Not only

[46] Center for the Study of Social Policy (2018). Strengthening families 101. https://cssp.org/resource/strengtheningfamilies101/

is it incredibly important information regarding the prevention of these ACEs, and therefore a lower risk for future health concerns, but it also speaks measures to the idea that health is not - cannot possibly be - just the things that are happening in, to, and with our bodies.

Throughout training, we are asked to calculate our own ACE scores. At one point, I thought mine was zero. After many years of therapy, I realized that in addition to my tendency to think in black in white, I also minimize my own experiences and emotions. It would be easy to say that my trauma developed with the traumatic loss and pain associated with watching my parents die, but that does not adequately represent my history.

In elementary school, I felt bullied. I do not remember anything specific that was said or done, but I do remember that one way I dealt with it was to write a short story. I tried to change the names to inconspicuous one, like Jane to June or Lindsey to Lonnie. I was so proud of my story and had grandiose dreams of getting it published. In retrospect, it was quite a healthy way to process my emotions - though it likely lacked substance and flow, since it was written by an eleven-year-old. What I remember specifically was showing my mom, who laughed at me. I do not even remember what she said, but I remember feeling ashamed and silly. I do not say that I was bullied because my mom's reaction and because both my mom and my tendency to minimize that often prevents me from recognizing it as an absolute.

I was often told not to make a mountain out of a molehill, or to not be so dramatic. I get it as a parent now. It is exhausting listening to a child complain about getting the blue cup instead of the green one. It is easy to try to compare their small world to the big world we live in and think that they have nothing to cry about. To my little dudes and to the little girl I once was, the pain and sadness experienced in that small way is very real and to their small worlds, very big. It is still deserving of validation. Because of this, for a long time I thought about my childhood experience as nothing. I could not figure out why I was the way I was when my childhood had been so "perfect".

My childhood was not perfect. My dad was a charismatic and kind man, loved by many. However, there were times when I was belittled or made fun of by him; where I did not feel worthy or enough; where I was told I was fat. It's likely his behavior was due to his own trauma experienced as a child, but that is not my story to tell. My dad drank alcohol to the social norm in our area. Unfortunately, the cultural norm is above the recommended level. It could also be argued that both my parents struggled with poor mental health. This is not to speak poorly of them. I, in no way, believe my parents intentionally caused me emotional harm or tried to minimize my feelings and experiences. Today I am a firm believer that we are all doing the best we can with what we have. That does not mean, however, that it did not impact me.

ACEs do not capture (1) the death of a parent; (2) being a caretaker of a younger sibling or parent; or (3) being in a family in which the primary breadwinner – or anyone for that matter - is diagnosed with a terminal illness. Knowing that ACEs can increase risks for heart disease, substance use and/or abuse, and depression, also leads me to believe that trauma and stress in general can have a negative impact on our mental and physical health.

As someone whose parents have both died on or before their 50th year on this earth from fatal illnesses, I think about health frequently. During the development of this book, I started exploring what health means to me. I started thinking about how I have obsessed over what I put into my body, the exercises and activity I engage in - should I do yoga, should I eat organic, should I feed my kids sugar - the thoughts are endless.

I remember talking to my brother one time about health habits - specifically, his chewing tobacco habit - and he said to me, "Brenna, mom and dad were pretty healthy people and they still died young. Don't you think we're just going to die when we're going to die?" Well with that attitude mister, you bet you are! But there is some truth to it. His laid-back approach, his seemingly effortless ability to remain calm and unaffected by whatever stress is thrown his way, is likely a much healthier approach than the mental stress I put on myself to be healthy.

I think of a conversation after my mother died in which someone told me they believed that my mom died because of the food and chemicals she put in her body. I do not think it was said in a blaming way, more as a theory. Years later at a conference, a woman presented on how a change in diet had saved her dad from terminal cancer. Sitting there I realized how much credit we give to people's choices and behaviors, when it could be perceived as blame if the results are poor. Any extreme stress over what we do or eat cannot possibly be great for our health.

I keep rereading a passage that asks, "do I really want to prevent myself from dying if it means giving up my life to 'live well'?" In the big picture, I can say a resounding "no." I would much rather spend my time, efforts and brainpower on living than on preventing death. While the medical world is making great strides in identifying how to prevent the flu, fight disease and prolong life, I would rather spend my time eating the chocolate, snuggling and watching a movie on the couch with my babies and doing what makes me feel good.

One thing I can say absolutely did not feel good was pregnancy and childbirth. Now, I am not saying I would take it back. I love my two boys with every cell of my being - mostly when they are sleeping and not crying - and the love is unconditional. I would not trade it for the world and I sure as hell am not putting them back where they came from. That shit hurt! I remember my mom telling me how beautiful pregnancy and childbirth was. She made it all seem so wonderful, peaceful... natural. I remember asking her if childbirth hurt, and if I would poop on the birthing table. She told me I would not care and that it would all be worth it.

Without her around for the pregnancy and birth of my children, I felt like I was doing it wrong. I was miserable throughout my pregnancy. I had cravings, I was too exhausted from growing a human to exercise and my sex drive did not increase like so many books and movies make you believe. I was dead set on having a natural, unmedicated birth. I read every book I could get my hands on and wrote a modest, 2-page birth plan which I shared with my providers and the hospital during my pre-admission visit weeks before labor and delivery. I did not want drugs; I did not want to be asked if I wanted drugs; I did not want drugs anywhere near me because I wanted to experience the beauty and miracle of raw childbirth.

That shit rocked my world. I was a great candidate for a natural birth - being low risk - and was assured many times by my providers. What I did not account for was that I was terrified and even though I have always been told I had a high pain tolerance, my body was singing a different tune.

I labored at home for as long as I could, based on best guess being 45 minutes away from the hospital. I was only dilated to a 2 when I got to the hospital. I progressed slowly and the nurse on staff said I was likely not to give birth before she left 6 hours later. I took that as a challenge as I do with most things. I started walking and moving and working at getting that baby moving down, down, down. Then my body started freaking out. I was puking in the garbage can. Everything hurt and I was scared. I panicked. My blood pressure skyrocketed.

I remember the doctor saying that I needed to lay down on my side to get my blood pressure to lower. She said more than once that I needed to consider pain medication, and I remember being terrified and mad. No, I did not want pain medication. She said the word pre-eclampsia and seizures. I kept saying no.

I remember screaming at the top of my lungs, but the people in the room did not witness that at all. Eventually I asked for something to dull the pain. No epidural but something. It was apparently a two-hour dose and in two hours I went from a 4 to a 10. I was begging for more when I felt that push that you would only recognize if you have had a baby. It is kind of like that feeling of needing to vomit, how your body convulses on its own. I pushed for less than 30 minutes and my little baby was placed on my chest. I kept asking, "what is it?" And nobody would answer me. It was probably only three minutes, but it felt like forever.

"It's a boy!"

And I loved him. I loved him when my body was growing him, and I loved him to the point I thought my heart would burst.

About 22 hours after my son was born, I mentioned to the nurse that we were planning to leave after the 24 hour24-hour point. So, we did. Childbirth is strange. It is a time which is so natural but feels anything but. Especially if you are in a hospital.

Hospitals are where sick people are. Hospitals are where my mom died. Hospitals are where people have surgeries, or where they don't, as my dad didn't before he was sent home to die. In the same hospital, in fact, where I delivered my two babies. I did not really make that connection before the first baby. I do know that I felt traumatized. I had nightmares that I was pregnant and was going to have to deliver a baby over and over. I was terrified, yet I knew I wanted to do it again.

When my oldest son approached his first birthday, I started considering it. I wanted him to have a sibling. I decided I would absolutely get an epidural and as many drugs that they would let me take to get the baby out as quickly and painlessly as possible. I started thinking about how to make this birth different.

I was surprised that it took me so long to connect my first traumatic birthing experience and to hear scary words about my health and risks to a hospital in which my mom had died. While other people may have known that her health was poor enough to die, I did not register it. I was shocked. It was like being punched in the stomach.

The day she died; I was at church. I had a dozen missed calls and text messages, telling me to get to the hospital. I was with my childhood friend. Somehow, I got behind the wheel and nearly killed us passing cars to get to the hospital. She was so near death when I got there. Her breathing was slow; her lips were dry. She asked for water and I wanted to give her some, and someone said, "it doesn't matter anymore, Brenna." A comment likely from their own hurt but something I have not forgotten about that day over ten years ago. Someone asked me if I wanted to be in the room when she died, and I could not. I walked out of the room with my arms around my brother. I found my family, collapsed to the floor, and lay my head on my friend's lap, sobbing.

My friend drove home from the hospital, and I made her listen to Taylor Swift's song "The Best Day" throughout the entire 45-minute drive. My world had stopped. The rest of the world kept going, but mine had stopped. Just like birth, when you welcome a new life into the world, your world stops. When you say goodbye to someone in death, your world stops. The similarities are eerie. The fact that I gave birth in the place in which I was so traumatized by losing my mother was certainly nothing to be ignored.

I started talking to my providers about how traumatized I was, and that I needed a different approach. I cried. I talked to a doctor about switching to a midwife as no offense to the doctors. I wanted to avoid a potential trauma of being with someone in a white coat that had once told me my mother was dying, that was now supposed to be helping me bring life into the world. It was not easy.

I had contractions on and off for weeks with my second son. Strong ones. Ones that I thought were real. I was in and out of the doctor's office, and had one false alarm visit to the hospital. When I was 39 weeks pregnant, my water broke at 3am. I knew it had broken and since I was not trying to labor at home this time, I started prepping for the day of my baby's arrival. My contractions slowed by the time we got to the hospital.

It took a couple of hours to even determine if my water had broken. Finally, after a nurse pushed a little strip of paper into the pad I was sitting on, and the strip turned purple, I received word that I had amniotic fluid on the bedsheets. My contractions were sporadic and not intensifying. They set me up in a room. The room was dark per my request, to avoid the bright hospital lights. I napped. I was relaxed and it was peaceful.

My midwife came in after about four hours and said, "well, how about we get you started with an epidural and then Pitocin and have a baby?" Once the epidural was in and my left leg was completely numb, they started the Pitocin. I giggled as the nurse noted my strong contractions, ones that I could not even feel. It was delightful.

It was such a different experience. I still felt pain. As my second baby pretty much shot down my cervix and birth canal, I started to feel the pressure, then the pain. I bet I felt about 50 minutes of pain. I asked what was happening because it was starting to hurt. The midwife reassured me that it was normal and, much to my chagrin, the epidural does not always numb everything. Seven minutes of pushing and two contractions and he was out. Umbilical cord still attached, I sat up and said, "that was awesome!" Because it was. It was so empowering, because I had made my needs known and asked for it to be better and my team helped me. It was not the natural birth I had imagined, but sometimes our strength comes from our willingness to be vulnerable. My team made my wishes come to life. It was like undoing the trauma of death, and transforming the hospital into a beautiful place of new life.

Growing a human provides a great picture of the many areas of health: a biological component taking place on a cellular level as cells multiply through mitosis; a hormonal component as the mother's hormone levels change; a physical component as the woman's body changes, her organs shift, her muscles stretch, and her joints loosen as she grows and prepares to birth the baby; and an emotional component, either good or bad, or maybe a little of both. Becoming a parent is joyful and terrifying. Considering giving your child up for adoption or terminating the pregnancy might be loving, guilt-producing, or exciting.

Pregnancy includes many pieces, and no two experiences are the same. The same could be said for what makes up our health. Some consider it to include physical, emotional, spiritual, and mental health.

One way we might categorize mental and physical health is based on measurability. Physical health is more measurable and more observable, whereas mental health includes more subjective and abstract symptoms. This is not to say that mental health is less real than physical health. The opposite is true, as mental health has been shown to affect physical health, such as the study on ACEs discussed earlier.

What is mental health, anyway? It seems to be like the giant Egyptian pyramids, made of thousands of pieces of limestone added together piece upon piece upon piece to create the overall structure. The United States Department of Health and Human Services defines it as including our emotional and psychological health, as well as social well-being as developed according to biological factors – such as genes or brain chemistry – life experiences – such as trauma or abuse – and family history of mental health problems. It is no surprise then that when completing a psychosocial assessment in the mental and behavioral health realm, that it includes the aforementioned, plus employment and education history, substance use and abuse and social supports and resources. While these things are not as tangible as a glucose reading or blood pressure, they can be quantified and combined to create a picture of someone's overall mental health.

As we move through life trying to maximize our health and expand our life, weight and body size tends to enter the picture. In addition to all the other pieces that make up our overall health, some believe there are specific weights and shapes our bodies should take in order to be considered healthy.

Body mass index (BMI), for example, is a person's weight in kilograms divided by the square of height in meters, and is said by the Centers for Disease Control and Prevention (CDC) to be strongly correlated with various metabolic and disease outcomes. For example, an individual that is five feet, five inches tall and weighs 170 pounds has a BMI of 28.3 and is considered overweight. The suggested weight range for someone of this height is between 111 and 150 pounds. The BMI does not consider that the last time I was at that weight range, I was wildly obsessed with every piece of food I put in my mouth and how many minutes I exercised. In extreme times at that weight, I was engaging in binging and purging or restricting my eating to unhealthy limits. BMI does not account for muscle mass or cardiovascular health. It has been suggested by many people to remove the tracking of BMIs entirely, as it fails to provide an accurate picture of a person's overall health.[47]

Some reject the idea of BMI so vehemently, that it is referenced as nothing but a myth generated by the CDC "fueled by the power of money and cultural bias."[47] Linda Bacon, author of Health at Every Size, proposes that the following are all myths generated by the CDC:

> Overweight and obesity lead to early death.
>
> Overweight and obesity lead to disease.
>
> We are gaining weight at epidemic rates.
>
> Weight loss improves health and longevity.
>
> You control what you weigh.
>
> Anyone can keep lost weight off if she or he tries hard enough.
>
> Thinner is more attractive.
>
> We can trust the experts to provide accurate information.

The HAES movement aims to advance social justice, create an inclusive and respectful community, and support people of all sizes in finding compassionate ways to take care of themselves. A number of different factors are hypothesized that might account for the relationship

---

[47] Bacon, L. (2008). Health at every size. Dallas, TX: BenBella Books.

between size and chronic health risks. For example, individuals who are larger are discriminated against more or are on the receiving end of looks and comments of disgust and therefore the emotional distress is the cause of poorer health outcomes. Or how a sedentary lifestyle may predispose someone to weight gain and make them more vulnerable to many diseases. HAES® contends it is well established that the relationship between activity and longevity is stronger than the relationship between weight and longevity.[47]

What I am saying is maybe it is more important to focus on the behaviors of both the person and our society, rather than the person's size. One of my favorite quotes from Bacon's Health At Every Size® book states,

"Because really, what's beneath your weight-loss quest? Isn't your ultimate goal to feel better about yourself, to feel love, acceptance, vitality, or good health?"[47]

Those things are not made from a mental illness, diet or one absolute size, it is made of many small moments and as such, so is your health.

Eating Disorders and Obesity

My mom used to tell me that I was "small but mighty." I was a petite little kiddo. The mixed messages that we receive in our society are funny. Are we eating too little; are we eating too much? If they are that little they must not be eating; if they are fat, they must be eating too much. What is with this obsession? Are we really nothing more than obsessing about our body sizes and what we look like? We as a society are obsessed with health, and there is nothing healthy about being obsessed with health. Studies show that there are a multitude of factors that affect our health such as psychological and emotional stress, that goes beyond how our bodies look.[48] Rather than asking ourselves, "do I feel unwell, do I move, do I feed my body nutrients, do I have energy?" we focus on the number on

[48] Bacon, L. (2008). Health at every size. Dallas, TX: BenBella Books.

the scale or the inches around the waist.

My oldest son is petite. When he was 12 months old, we started to notice he was not growing anymore. The kid could put away at least one, but sometimes two full bratwursts at one meal. He was a great eater, and nothing was sticking. Without my mom here to talk to and ask questions about my development, it is hard to tell if my kiddo gets it from me – if she had a similar experience with the fear of not knowing if something was wrong with me; if she lost sleep over the fear that people were judging her for not caring for her child.

Over the course of the next couple months, his growth had completely stunted, and he dropped off the charts. We had numerous doctor's appointments in which we would report day after day of food diaries. At one point, a colleague of our son's pediatrician told us to feed him as much fat as we could, "anything you think you're supposed to avoid, give it to him... put butter on everything!" So we did. We allowed him to eat whatever he wanted, whenever he wanted, wherever he wanted. And that was frustrating. Some days he would just eat pack upon pack of fruit snacks. In hindsight, I know that is not healthy or nutritious. I just wanted the kid to put on some weight.

On more than one occasion, his pediatrician suggested that our son may have Celiac disease. I was familiar with the disease because of an uncle that also had it. The pediatrician explained that people with Celiac disease who continue to eat gluten end up triggering an immune response that damages their intestines and prevents their bodies from absorbing nutrients. She ordered a blood draw.

After holding down our squirmy 13-month-old for a blood draw by two completely capable phlebotomists and only shedding a few tears - between my son, my husband and me - we received the results that the test was inconclusive. The pediatrician then ordered an endoscopy and a colonoscopy. There is nothing exciting about those words and as terrible as I thought it would be, I was right. I wanted to hold my baby as they gave him the anesthesia for the test. It, honest to goodness, felt like he had died right there in my arms. Thankfully, the tests did not take long, and it was less than an hour later that we were taken back to our baby's hospital room.

After a couple of weeks of waiting for the results, they were explained again as inconclusive. After some back and forth, we were instructed to just "try" the gluten free diet. Let me just say, I was terrified. I hated those instructions. I was not just worried that I would not be able to keep the gluten away from my kiddo. I knew that "gluten free" for someone with Celiac did not just mean we had to watch what he ate but watch for cross-contamination as well. I knew that it meant he would not be able to eat at the majority of restaurants, daycare or school. Those things I knew - and knew we could handle.

What I was most afraid of was the judgment from other people. I was afraid to be "that mom" who would not let her kid eat gluten. "But it is not my choice!" I would think. I spoke with a family member at the time and she said, "fuck them. Why would it matter what others' think?" What I am realizing now is that the reason it mattered what other people thought is because I think judgmental thoughts about other people and their eating habits. It is awful and I am ashamed to admit it. I hear someone say, "I don't eat gluten and don't let my little Suzy eat it either," and I think "oh for the love of God just eat the food!" Who am I to think that? Have I not also struggled with an eating disorder? It has been suggested that obsession with healthy foods such as avoiding gluten is a type of disordered eating called orthorexia.[49] If I were to think with compassion and empathy about others' obsessions, I might have responded differently to changing our kiddo to a gluten-free lifestyle. I likely would not have felt so afraid of the looks and judgments I feared would come my way.

After my first few days of fear, several conversations with my husband that may have been construed as denial, and so much sanitizing of our kitchen utensils and appliances, we were gluten free. And after a couple months? Our little dude grew two inches and gained four pounds and was right back on track with his growth. The experience helped me realize that if I needed to do something to make my kid healthier, I just needed to do it. It also helped me be a bit more compassionate when I saw others restraining from certain foods; rather than looking on with annoyance, I reminded myself I have no idea what that person is dealing with.

---

[49] National Eating Disorder Association (2018). Orthorexia. Retrieved from https://www.nationaleatingdisorders.org/learn/by-eating-disorder/other/orthorexia

Even after my kid was back on his growth curve, he continued to be small. My husband frequently talked about his fear that our son would be small. This is a stereotype in itself – that boys and men should be big – and we had many talks about that. While still trying to validate my husband's fears, I would say how that concern might impose on our kid that his body has to be a certain size or shape.

We talked to the pediatrician about his growth and she assured us it was normal. During one conversation my husband and I admitted that we felt as though we made many good parenting decisions and at the same time struggled with supporting our child's eating habits. We told her about our philosophy to let him eat whatever, whenever, wherever – stemming from the times when he was not growing.

At this point, our son's pediatrician told us about the work of Ellyn Satter, who wrote many pieces of work on feeding children and families.[50] She said we could determine how much, where, when, and what our son would eat, but we could not determine whether or not he *would*. This resonated with me. Not for my own sake – like, "oh yea I should listen to my body when it's hungry or full like a child would," – but rather a trust in my kiddo to listen to his body when he is hungry or full.

Through continued research into Ellyn Satter's work (and trust me, this is still a work in progress), I learned

---

[50] Satter, E. (2019). The Ellyn Satter Institute. Retrieved from https://www.ellynsatterinstitute.org/

that it is my job to raise competent eaters, not healthy eaters. The way I interpret that is: It is my job to empower my children to make decisions regarding what they eat and how they move that makes their bodies feel good, focusing more on how they feel and less on how they look.

For the most part, I would say that my husband is good at understanding his own cues of hunger and fullness. For some reason, though, he has continued to struggle with trusting our son to determine whether or not he would eat. We continue to have conversations about avoiding phrases like, "you have to have 12 more bites of this food," or, "his eating sucks," or, "he needs to eat more." On one level, I have heard this is a completely normal point of anxiety for many parents - "am I feeding my kid enough?" - and on another level, it seems we have been pushed to another dimension of worry due to his size. And there we have it: more obsession with size. Is he big enough, too big, too small, too lumpy?

This is not surprising for someone like me. Frankly, it is not surprising for someone who lives in the world that we do. Our culture is obsessed with the size of our bodies. At one level, it makes sense. Our bodies are the vessels in which we live during our time here on earth, and therefore it makes sense that we would find out everything we can to take the best possible care of them. What it means to take care of our bodies is a source of great debate, however.

I know that depriving myself of food and obsessing over what I eat is not taking care of myself. I am in recovery from an eating disorder. I am not really even sure why I say that or if I am using the phrase correctly. We have a picture in our minds of what a person with an eating disorder looks like, and I did not look like that. I was not "all skin and bones," I did not lose my period, and I never got feedback like, "you need to eat something, you're too skinny!"

I grew up in a house with very complex attitudes about food. On my dad's side, food was, and still is equated to love. We love to cook it and to eat it. On my mother's side, food is a necessity but is generally something we avoid. We eat it to live but should not get fat.

I received complicated messages about my body growing up. I was always told I was beautiful. I am learning now that message in itself is complicated. If we grow up in a place that is constantly sending us messages about our bodies and our appearance, we place an unwarranted amount of value on those external qualities. I remember being told by a doctor at age 14, "you are so pretty, you could be a Hollister model or something." Sounds nice, right? Or maybe creepy. Or maybe completely inappropriate, irrelevant and even if I was over 18, none of his damn business to be commenting about what I could be doing with my body.

When I was younger, I was a dancer. My first ballet lessons predate my memories of them. I started when I was three and danced until I was 12. At the time, I quit because I did not like the commitment. I wanted to play with my friends. It was not cool to dance.

Looking back at it now, I wonder if the time I quit had more to do with the fact that I was entering puberty. Ballet taught me great posture. It taught me how to suck in my belly just right because tights and leotards show everything. It taught me to be the best I could be and always "keep face."

Ballet classes are taught in a room full of mirrors, presumably, so you can watch your form. I suspect they are about watching your body size as well. I am not sure if I thought this or overheard an adult say it, but I remember looking at the older ballet dancers and thinking the skinny ones were so beautiful and graceful and the heavier and larger breasted women looked awkward and out of place. I stopped dancing at twelve, which means these experiences and thoughts all predated that time.

My mother was a small woman. Many people told me how similar I was to her. I was constantly compared to her, and my older sister was constantly compared to my dad: she had the long thin legs while my mother and I were both shorter and petite. I remember my dad telling me at my mom's heaviest, whilst pregnant; she weighed 148 pounds. When he told me that, I had yet to reach that weight, and I did not think I ever would. If she could stay below that, so would I.

My mom tried hard to teach us positive body image, like how she tried to teach us that being a woman would not hold me back. Unfortunately, what she modeled was vastly different than what she said. She would often police food; we were not allowed to have many sugary snacks or cereals. I felt shame if I wanted it. When we are forced to avoid something, it is all we want. I remember being a young kid, maybe 10 or 11 and shoving three cookies in my mouth at once to hide them from my mom.

It is not a surprise I would hide food and binge. My mom used to have a secret chocolate stash. At the time I thought it was so none of us would eat it. That may have been partly true, but it may have had more to do with the shame she felt from desiring to eat the tasty chocolate, stemming from the confusing messages of food and body size from her family.

As I entered my teenage years, my waist and hips stayed slim, and my breasts grew large. Whenever I reflect on this time people will say, "so you had the perfect body?" That seems funny because I never remember feeling I had the perfect body. I was always running, eating something different, striving to be smaller. Even before my teenage years I remember sitting and pinching my stomach fat between my thumb and forefinger and thinking, "if only I could just slice this whole thing off with a knife, I would look good." I never made the connection that "looking good" was synonymous with "being happy" in my eyes.

One thing that complicated fitness and nutrition further was that movement and exercise meant more to me than a smaller body. Despite confusing messages I received that we exercised to control our weight, it also helped me feel good. I have struggled with depression since I was 14 and when I was on an exercise routine, it tended to combat the depression. Unfortunately, as a person that struggles with polarized thought, it also meant I beat myself up if I did not stick to my regime.

When I was a senior in high school, I remember standing in the kitchen with my mom and her saying, “maybe you need to start working out again.” My mother exhibited disordered eating patterns and held negative feelings towards larger body size and shape. Although I cannot remember the context of our conversation, for many years I assigned this memory to the start of my eating disorder – over-exercising, anorexia and then bulimia. Over time I started to give her the benefit of the doubt. It is possible she was suggesting I exercise to feel good because exercise makes me feel good – period. Isn’t it strange the memories we have and how they are able to influence our beliefs? For years, I allowed that memory to significantly impact the way in which I engaged in what I thought was healthy activity and dieting.

In college, the year after my mom died, I decided to become a vegetarian. That was my rule, to not eat meat, and it was a strange one considering I was raised on venison burgers and squirrel soup. The obsession I had over this restriction game me a sense of control and created disordered eating that is obvious to me now. At the time, I just thought it was healthy.

For hundreds – if not thousands – of years, professionals have been studying the body for causes of disease and sources of increasing longevity. Increasing longevity is an interesting topic of its own – why live longer? Why not just live better, perhaps happier?

One thing that has been proposed is that our beliefs about the negative correlation between obesity and health may put us at risk in another way. Cross-cultural studies suggest that larger people are not subject to the same diseases in countries where there is less stigma attached to weight.[48] So, in places such as the United States, where judgment and prescriptions of mortality come with bigger bodies, larger people experience poorer mental health. And where there is poorer mental health, there is poorer physical health.

Further it has been identified that there is a stronger relationship between BMI, and disease and early death, among groups more negatively affected by body image concerns.[48] When researchers looked at a representative group of more than 170,000 adults in the United States, they found the difference between actual weight and perceived ideal weight was a better indicator of mental and physical health than BMI. In other words, as said in Linda Bacon's book Health at Every Size®, "Feeling fat has stronger health effects than being fat."48 Bacon asserts that the only way we can solve the weight problem, is to stop judging ourselves and others by size. She says it so darn well, "Weight is not an effective measure of attractiveness, moral character, or health. The real enemy is weight stigma, for it is the stigmatization and fear of fat that causes the damage and deflects attention from true threats to our health and well-being..."[48]

It is a fallacy to believe we can control our weight in the first place. One definitively controversial area is dieting.

Everywhere we look a new diet is being offered. I need to be clear that I do not write about any of this from a point of judgment or up on a pedestal looking down. I speak of many diets from personal experience, situations where I have restricted myself or given myself rules time and time again, only to think worse of myself for failing to lose the weight.

The thing is, according to Health at Every Size®, our bodies are made in such a way that dieting is harmful and only minimally works. What dieting does do: Slows the rate at which your body burns calories; increases your body's efficiency at wringing every possible calorie out of the food you do eat so you digest food faster and get hungrier quicker; causes you to crave high-fat foods; increases your appetite; reduces your energy levels so even if you could burn more calories through physical activity you don't want to in order to preserve your energy; lowers your body temperature so you are using less energy and are always cold; reduces your ability to feel "hungry" and "full," making it easier to confuse hunger with emotional needs; reduces your total amount of muscle tissue; and increases fat-storage enzymes and decreases fat-release enzymes.[48]

If you are like me and tend to take information and create a new rule for yourself, let me just stop you right there. Flexibility is far more important than any one rule either in support of or against dieting. If a rubber band becomes cold and rigid, it snaps. You do not need food rules – what so many think of as a diet – to guide your choices, and you do not need to fight against what you really want. All we need to do is listen to our body and respond to what it says. Pay attention to how you feel after you binge on a dozen cookies - I for one do not feel the greatest when I do that.

I tend to feel better when I drink a lot of water and eat a good combination of proteins, fats and carbohydrates. I do not need to create a rule or track every calorie though; I can remind myself what is likely to make me feel the best the next time I am hungry. Sometimes what makes me feel best is eating ice cream for dinner. Sometimes it is the frozen pizza after a long day because I do not have the energy to prepare a meal.

It would be too easy to say this all speaks only to women. Frankly, that would be sexist and disregard the impact on men. There has been an increase in the number of men being afflicted with issues formerly associated with women such as eating disorders, body obsessions, and low physical self-esteem. In fact, Cornell researchers found that men and women are similarly dissatisfied with their weight, despite variations in men and women's ideas of a desirable appearance. Men tend to want to have more muscle definition and mass whereas women tended to want to lose weight.[51]

This all speaks to what an absolute obsession we have with the body, and why there are two highly prevalent related issues right now: obesity and diets.

---

[51] Cornell University. "Most college students wish they were thinner, study shows." ScienceDaily. ScienceDaily, 21 November 2007. Retrieved from www.sciencedaily.com/releases/2007/11/071120111544.htm.

According to the Centers for Disease Control and Prevention (CDC), more than one-third (36.5%) of U.S. adults are considered obese.[52] Studies have shown time and again that there is a positive correlation between obesity and a number of health conditions.[53] I get it, I am not a doctor or anything, but research presented in Health at Every Size® has shown that focus on weight (loss, gain, obesity) may not be the be-all, end-all, cure-all for medical issues. Rather, the focus on behaviors – which are commonly associated with smaller bodies – such as eating more fruits and vegetables, drinking water, getting moderate exercise may improve health conditions.

Think about it for a second. If you were to picture your idea of a healthy individual, what does that look like? Probably someone with a small build. We associate size with health, but is that entirely accurate? When asked if "fat people deserve to be happy," people often respond by saying, "if they're healthy." Would you say that about a skinny person? Who is to say that a fat person who runs 10 miles a week is not healthier than a skinny person who smokes a pack of cigarettes a day? Unfortunately, we live in a society that places worth on body size, creating an unhealthy place to live and exist.

---

[52] Ogden, C.L., et. al (2015). Prevalence of obesity among adults and youth: United States, 2011-2014. NCHS data brief, *No. 219*

[53] National Heart, Lung and Blood Institute (2013). Why obesity is a health problem. Retrieved from https://www.nhlbi.nih.gov/health/educational/wecan/healthy-weight-basics/obesity.htm

Consider the type of food we eat. What has processed food done to our health? Is it possible that the food we are eating in terms of chemicals and processing are the causes of fatness, and not how much of that food we are eating? If the more processed foods are less expensive and have a higher shelf life - maybe someone can only go grocery shopping once every two weeks when paid, or once a month when they receive their food assistance money - that is what people at a lower socio-economic status will eat.

It has been reported that in developing countries, the higher the socioeconomic status, the higher the risk for obesity. In developed countries, the results are much more confusing. Race and gender play a role in the difference of risk for obesity. For men, the risk of obesity appears to be consistent across all races. Some studies have shown that a trend may exist for black or Hispanic men, where those that are higher on the socio-economic scale are also at a higher risk for obesity. Women also tend to have a similar risk across SES, with white woman showing a higher risk for obesity when they are lower on the socioeconomic scale. The risk for obesity cannot be simply summarized by saying, if you are poor, you are more likely to be obese and if you are rich you are less likely.[54]

If the socioeconomic scale correlation to obesity is inaccurate, what is causing it? Perhaps it is our culture

---

[54] Centers for Disease Control and Prevention (2010). Obesity and socioeconomic status in adults: United states 2005-2008. Retrieved from https://www.cdc.gov/nchs/data/databriefs/db50.pdf

and the foods we are attracted to that lead to obesity. Perhaps it is the ideal body sizes among different cultures, that pressure people to be attracted to food that makes our bodies become bigger or smaller. Or perhaps - stay with me here - some bodies are simply different than other bodies.

Health At Every Size®, proposes what some may call a radical theory about the body and diet culture. Based on scientifically tested and published research, Bacon proposes that 1) diets simply do not work; 2) health can be achieved regardless of weight; and 3) our bodies have their own set weight that they will return to time and time again, despite weight loss efforts. Further she proposes that bodies can be healthy at each individual set weight if healthy behaviors are engaged in, regardless if the number on the scale ever moves. When I first started looking into the Health at Every Size® lifestyle I thought, “sweet, Reese's peanut butter cups for breakfast, lunch and dinner!” And that is what I did for a while.

What I was missing was inhabiting the full spirit of Health at Every Size® in which we engage in healthy behaviors that help our bodies to work to the best of their abilities. Those behaviors should include things like fruits, vegetables, exercise, and yes, enjoying a treat every once in a while.

It is comical really, because like all other times in my life, I took on the Health At Every Size® culture in full storm saying, “Reese’s taste good so that is all I’m going to eat!” When I sit back and think about it, the healthiest approach we can take is one in which we consider what types of behaviors help us feel healthy (e.g., walking the dog, playing with the kids, eating a carrot with a dessert afterward) and then doing those things. What makes it healthy is when we can engage in those behaviors and then acknowledge that we are healthy, regardless of our body size.

In Andie Mitchell's memoir, "It Was Me All Along," she records her personal growth and enlightenment toward acceptance of self at any size. Much of the book resonated with me but there were two parts that felt like she reached right into the memory part of my brain and put into words what I could not.

> "Eating made me forget. The flavors, textures, and smells entertained me enough to mute my other senses. Filling my belly stuffed my mind so completely that no space existed for sadness. Packing myself with sweets until I ached created a new sensation, one that had nothing to do with intense loneliness and broken dads".
>
> I know that when I felt better physically, I was more motivated to eat well. The thought of potentially undoing any of the hard work I had put into walking and running weakened the appeal of bingeing. It became increasingly easier to choose healthy, wholesome foods and to keep my portions of rich indulgent foods small. For the first time in my life, I was able to eat decadently without gorging. Pasta, bread, pastries – all could

be eaten within reason".[55]

Andie's shift in attitude and behaviors may seem unattainable, but I remain hopeful. Health at Every Size® and the body positivity movement is seeking to change the way our culture looks at health, body shapes and sizes, and to promote the acceptance of the many diverse bodies that inhabit our world.

Despite the information out there, the Health at Every Size® principles have not been fully accepted into popular culture. Think about how many times in a day you see an advertisement for weight loss, an article on "how to get rid of the mom flab," or advertisements objectifying the usually female body. What these things tell us is, "look like me and you'll be happy/cool/worthy/loved too." In fact, the body positivity and Health at Every Size® movement has been accused of promoting obesity, whatever that means. From where I am sitting, what is being encouraged here is that all bodies are worthy, regardless of size.

We are able to control whether or not we engage in healthy behaviors. We are not able to control a much larger problem: the issue lies in the idea that the size of our body is somehow related to our morality: that if I am skinny, I am good, and if I am fat, I am bad.

When I was in the worst of my eating disorder, I was doing at least two hours of cardio a day, eating far too few calories and binging and purging, and I was not

---

[55] Mitchell, A. (2015). It was me all along: A memoir. New York, NY: Clarkson Potter.

happy. I was at my smallest, and still not happy. I think about the relationships I was in when I was a tiny little thing and I was not happy. I always thought I needed to lose more. I never had a boyfriend tell me I needed to lose weight or look different. I was the one with the problem with my body. Not others. I did not come up with the idea on my own though; it is something we are taught.

When we say the word *phobia*, we are really saying that we have an extreme or irrational fear of something. I have seen it used in so many ways from a specific phobia as a mental health diagnosis or as intense or severe anxiety to homophobia; a dictionary defined fear of homosexuality or an individual who is gay, albeit a mental disorder diagnosis.

It was not until recently that I started hearing the word fatphobia. The word fatphobia has yet to make it into dictionaries; currently only defined on urban dictionary and Wikipedia. It is however, a frequently used term in the Body Positivity culture. When I think about the word *fat* and then think about the word phobic meaning a severe or intense fear, I cannot help but think it is something I have been for many years. I was taught at a young age what foods would provide needed nutrients and I have remained active to one level or another. Regardless, I have always thought I was fat and for as long as I can remember I have engaged in behaviors to avoid being fat. I have always had fat, yes, and I have paired with it this sense of moral evilness in which I was bad because I had fat.

Recently, I started learning that I cannot see and believe these things about myself without posing the same judgments about other people around me. That is an incredibly unbecoming realization to come to and one that I am not proud of. In recent years, specifically since becoming a mother, I have put a good deal of energy into lifting others up. There was a time, at the beginning of my eating disorder in which I would vocally judge other women based on their size. I remember having a conversation with a friend in which she said, "if she can get a boyfriend so can I; look how fat she is!" I agreed. Probably because on the inside I felt so terrible about myself that I thought if I stepped on someone else, it would lift me up higher. On the outside, this was pure fat-shaming as a result of my fatphobia. That memory leaves me feeling embarrassed, ashamed and sad. If I think those things about others – "she's so fat so she doesn't deserve a boyfriend" – then I was feeling those things about myself too. Judging others for the size of their body is just not who I want to be.

Fatphobia and the obsession with others' body size is rampant. It is amazing how people feel the right to comment on bodies: whether positively or negatively. I remember going to the gym frequently with a workout buddy. At one point she said to me, "I should wear a bikini to the beach. Who cares what I look like? You have a belly, and you wear a bikini to the beach." I am not sure if she meant that as a compliment like, "we should not care what people think," but I will tell you that it burned in my brain as a moment of pure shame over wearing that two-piece bathing suit. After having my first baby and losing the baby weight, a male coworker said to me, "wow you're getting skinny. I kind of miss you being chubby." I was flattered at first that he noticed my hard work paying off. As I reflected later, I thought, why would he think he has the right to comment on my body? And oh my - do not get me started on body comments while pregnant. And oh my - do not get me started on body comments while pregnant. What is it about being pregnant, that people think they can say how beautiful/big/huge/swollen I am?

Our obsession with the size of our and others' bodies is far unhealthier than actually being fat. There are serious dichotomous themes in our society in which many are affected by eating disorders due to unrealistic body types displayed in media and the raging obsession with obesity. When we place worth on body size, we put pressure on fat people that can lead to stress. It results in shame for people with fat bodies or disordered eating. National surveys estimate that 20 million women and 10 million men in America will have an eating disorder at some point in their lives.[56]

It has also been concluded that people who are considered overweight may not seek medical attention for fear of being fat-shamed or misdiagnosed (e.g., "lose weight then we can talk about other options"). One woman I know was experiencing pain in her heel that was found to be the result of a bone spur. Her doctor

---

[56] National Eating Disorder Association (2018). Orthorexia. Retrieved from https://www.nationaleatingdisorders.org/learn/by-eating-disorder/other/orthorexia

recommended she first lose weight and then they would look at alternative treatment options. While my first response is to nod my head along, I quickly think, "wait, if she loses weight then the bony growth in her foot is just going to disappear?"

Consider the rise of weight-loss surgeries. We now have a procedure - gastric bypass or bariatric surgery - in which your body is physically altered in order to make you eat less and therefore fit into society's standards of a healthy weight range. The number of weight-loss surgeries performed in the U.S. grew by 450% from 1998 to 2002 and continues to increase in frequency today.[57] This is baffling to me, because studies have shown a number of side effects including increase in suicide, malnutrition, bowel obstruction, and death.[58] Additionally, long-term studies of the effects of weight-loss surgeries show that in the majority of cases, the weight comes back on.[59] I am certain the development of this procedure was based on the health issues the person was experiencing outweighing the risk of the surgery. However, I am hard-pressed to believe that this surgery - in which your stomach and intestine are severed in order for food to bypass most of your stomach, resulting

---

[57] Chang, L. (2005). Weight loss surgeries on the rise: Less-invasive techniques spur increase in bariatric surgery. Retrieved from https://www.webmd.com/diet/news/20051219/weight-loss-surgeries-on-rise

[58] MedicineNet (2015). Suicide risk may rise for some after weight-loss surgery. Retrieved from https://www.medicinenet.com/script/main/art.asp?articlekey=191076

[59] National Eating Disorder Association (2018). Orthorexia. Retrieved from https://www.nationaleatingdisorders.org/learn/by-eating-disorder/other/orthorexia

in decreasing the amount of food you can eat at one sitting and therefore reducing absorption of nutrients – is the solution to the number of health issues that plague our society today.

Please do not read this as me saying those people should have known better. It is possible that it was their last hope. Plus, people who have this surgery should not be expected to know something they could not know. It is not their job to identify the most safe and effective way to address their medical issues; that is the responsibility of their medical providers.

Perhaps weight loss surgery is the only option. That is a shame for large associations that are tasked with ensuring adequate research and information about promoting health, such as the Centers for Disease Control and Prevention and the National Institutes of Health. It is heartbreaking that corporations such as pharmaceutical companies benefit from people staying sick. It is infuriating that companies that financially benefit are also the same entities that fund health studies. Imagine how gravely distorted the information is that we receive regarding what is healthy or unhealthy for us. The prevalence of obesity and eating disorders in our society, as well as our overall obsession with health, is an issue resulting in a multitude of problems at legal, corporate, community, and personal levels.

With these many considerations, I have been able to acknowledge that the happiest and saddest points of my life are independent of my weight and size. Life is about so much more than the size of my body and the size of the bodies around me. I am learning that finding self-actualization – something that will bring lifelong joy, and likely not related to the size of my body – is what will make me happy. Not when I'm ___ pounds or a size ___.

I encourage you to contemplate your view of these issues and what type of judgment you may bring on yourself and others. If we want to live in a world that reduces the pressure of having a specific body type and size, we have to create it with each tiny moment we are presented with, each decision we make and each rule we choose to make or break.

Education and Experience

When I was growing up, I knew I was going to get a higher education. My mom also talked in the form of "when" we went to college, not "if." This does not count the time in preschool when I proclaimed otherwise. During our preschool graduation, I stood up in front of the church with my young peers and the teacher asked us each what we wanted to be when we grew up. My mom used to tell the story saying that my classmates professed desires to be doctors, firemen, teachers. I stood up there, all 36 inches of me, and yelled, "I want to be a pig!" My mom would say she wanted to crawl underneath her chair and hide. I find the story adorable, but I digress.

I am assuming my proclamation of wanting to be a pig had nothing to do with the fact that my mother encouraged us to go to college. I know that she frequently talked about wanting to give us a better life than she claimed to have had growing up. She would describe the holidays during her childhood in which she would feel grateful for the one gift she received while we begged and cried for more.

My mom grew up as the baby of four siblings. Growing up, her parents were farmers and still live in the same house they have lived in for over sixty years. They live a modest life and likely did provide a smaller Christmas celebration than what I experienced as a child. The wealth of my mother's childhood is likely a matter of opinion. My mother's parents are now in their eighties and continue to run their farm. My grandmother sends cards for every birthday and holiday. She tells me she loves me. That is a pretty rich way to live, in its own way.

In thinking of that now, my mom could have just been telling us not to be such spoiled little brats. One year for Christmas I said I wanted a specific gray kitten from a family friend's cat's recent litter. My letter to Santa said, "the grey kitten or nothing at all!" Looking back, I can see why she would say what she did. It seemed to go beyond that though. She would tell that story before explaining why it was so important to her to make the holidays really special, with overflowing stockings and presents from Santa. She was a supporter of the "treat yo'self" mentality, and would encourage us to do so anytime we needed a pick-me-up. Basically, what I learned was that having money and being able to obtain things was the way to show love and feel loved. I somehow also concluded that in order to have money, you needed an education.

It was not just what my mother said that made me want to go to school; it was watching her. When my brother, sister and I were in junior high, high school, and college, my mom was working three jobs and going to school. At that time, she seemed like superwoman. As a mother now, I am learning that there are more important things than killing myself over making money and finding ways to get more money.

That does not mean I do not value my education, nor does it mean I regret the years and dollars I put into my degrees. I have a voracious love for learning and a strong desire to keep going. If it is not a degree in higher education, I am seeking trainings or books, anything to learn more. My dad thought it was a waste. He would probably say the same now that I am pursuing my master's degree in business administration. I can almost hear him say, "Jesus, what a waste of time and money!" When I was getting my master's in social work, he frequently told me what a waste it was, and how education was unnecessary to make money.

There are a couple reasons I think my dad had the opinions on education that he did. I have a memory from when I was in elementary school, laying on my parents' bed with my dad and sister. He was reading a book and kept messing up the words and I remember thinking, "how come he doesn't know how to read?" Later, I learned that he had dyslexia. It is possible that his negative outlook on education started out of necessity to protect one of his shortcomings. He didn't need advanced education and he could make it on his own.

My dad was a prime example of the American dream. The story I was told was that he He grew up in a blue-collar family, in a small town in the northern lower peninsula of Michigan. When he was 16, during his senior year of high school, his parents moved to the Detroit area following one of many traumatic family experiences. I always thought he stayed in his hometown My dad decided to stay in a little town with his older brothers, though later learned his brothers had entered the Navy that year and he stayed behind without his family. He graduated high school and went on to purchase a landscaping company. My dad and mom grew that company over the course of 25 years, to include both landscaping and irrigation. It was a successful business, made possible by his 80-hour work weeks, salesman charm, business savvy and my mom's support. With a success story like his, I get why that too could contribute to suspicion of a desire for education.

Education and experience can both move us forward. I remember hearing in both my undergraduate and graduate programs that the majority of useful tools and applicable knowledge would be things I would learn on the job. I soaked up as much education as I could - with the occasional hangover or booty call thrown in. School taught me how to ask questions, how to research, how to write, and how to communicate. Schooling was humbling. Even spending six years in school full-time, I can say with certainty that in the same time on the job, I have learned just as much through experience.

Because of my experience with my parents and with my education, I can appreciate both sides of the experience versus education argument. I would not want one without the other. I can see how others are able to pull themselves up by their bootstraps, how the school of hard knocks can be an education in itself. A trade school education without massive amounts of debt is nothing to dismiss. It just would not let me accomplish what I wanted to accomplish. As Amy Poehler writes in her book Yes, Please, "good for you, not for me."[60] I am grateful for both sides of the coin, and I would not want to miss out on either one. With all or nothing thinking, it can feel that way. You can decide that if one is important, the other must not be. The spectrum of education and experience is not really a spectrum at all. They are two valuable factors that can add to a life of success.

There is a large variety of educational opportunities out there, ranging from formal to informal, in-person to online, plus tuition-based classes, certifications, and books and other materials. The level of accessibility to education depends greatly on the community you grew up in, the school that prepared you for higher education, the family that set expectations and the dreams and goals you have. Without a desire to have a career that utilizes a college education, the rest is all moot. Without the proper resources, attaining your goal may be less possible. I am not going to pretend to be anything but the white, middle-ish class woman I am. I know that I

---

[60] Poehler, Amy (2015). Yes Please. New York, NY: Dey Street Books.

am privileged in many ways. Despite this, or perhaps because of it, I know that my life might have been entirely different if I had been born into a different family, in a different community, with differently colored skin.

Many studies show a correlation of socioeconomic status and race with education with some breath-catching statistics:

> Dropout rates of 16 to 24-years-old students who come from low-income families, show individuals in this population are seven times more likely to drop out than those from families with higher incomes.[61]
>
> By the end of the 4th grade, African-American, Hispanic and low-income students, on average, are already 2 years behind grade level. By the time they reach the 12th grade they are 4 years behind.[62]
>
> A higher percentage of young adults (31%) without a high school diploma live in poverty, compared to the 24% of young people who

---

[61] Ramani, K., et al. (2014). Trends in High School dropout and completion rates in the United States: 1972-2009. *NCES*, 2019(117).

[62] Campbell, J., Hombo, C., & Mazzeo, J. (2014). Trends in Academic Progress. NAEP, 1999. US Department of Education, National Center for Education Statistics. Retrieved from https://nces.ed.gov/nationsreportcard/pubs/main1999/2000469.asp

> finished high school.[63]
>
> Less than 30% of students in the bottom quarter of incomes enroll in a 4-year school. Among that group - less than 50% graduate.[64]

While it is believed that education is the most powerful way to reduce poverty and improve health, gender equality, peace, and stability, not all individuals have equal access to it.[63]

In the past 20 years, the average tuition and fees at private U.S. universities have increased 168 percent. Out-of-state tuition and fees at public universities have risen 200 percent. In-state tuition and fees at public universities have grown the most, increasing 243 percent.[65] On average, college is currently costing around $29,500 per year and that is estimated to rise to around $110,000 per year in the next 20 years.[66]

The good news is that you have a cosigner and someone

---

[63] Children International (2019). Global poverty and education: Facts & stats about world poverty and education. Retrieved from https://www.children.org/global-poverty/global-poverty-facts/facts-about-world-poverty-and-education.

[64] Deparle, Jason. (2014). "For Poor, Leap to College Often Ends in a Hard Fall." The New York Times. Retrieved from http://www.nytimes.com/2012/12/23/education/poor-students-struggle-as-class-plays-a-greater-role-in-success.html?pagewanted=all

[65] U.S. News (2018) See 20 years of tuition growth at national universities. Retrieved from https://www.usnews.com/education/best-colleges/paying-for-college/articles/2017-09-20/see-20-years-of-tuition-growth-at-national-universities

[66] College Calc (2019). Savings plan and future cost estimation. Retrieved from http://www.collegecalc.org/calculators/plan and save/?age=0&cost=29500

telling you how important college is – rather than working multiple jobs to make ends meet – you can sell your soul to the United States government for loans at a steep 7.5-8% annual percentage rate. The current student loan debt in the United States is estimated at around $1.53 trillion with the average individual student loan debt around $37,172.[67] My loan is climbing quickly after attending a private university; I have accumulated tons of debt that I cannot even cover the interest on, even if I made three times the amount of money I am currently making.

It was my decision to attend a private university in order to join the workforce more quickly. While the government charges a pretty penny to have your education loaned to you, they do provide some programs for individuals who have these types of loans. I am able to participate in income-based repayment. If I do that for the next ten years while working at a qualifying agency such as a non-profit, my loan debt will be forgiven. Pending, of course, no changes to the Public Service Loan Forgiveness (PSLF) program.

Because my debt is higher than your average mortgage, I prioritize keeping track of my PSLF eligibility so that before I am 35, I will have my student loans paid off. This is a much better deal than most folks, who literally take their whole life to pay off their student debt. What if I was unaware of PSLF? What if I was trying day in

---

[67] Nitro College (2019). Average student loan debt in the U.S.: 2019 Statistics. Retrieved from https://www.nitrocollege.com/research/average-student-loan-debt

and day out just to survive? If I was focused on ensuring my basic needs were met and that I could get health care when I needed it, it is very likely that a program like this would be lower on my awareness level.

I have lived a privileged life thus far, and have not faced overt discrimination. If I were black and were to defy the odds of graduating high school, how might the discrimination I face provide an additional barrier to completing college? If I were born into a lower socioeconomic status, what are the chances I would be keeping track of how to access loans, grants, scholarships and potentially loan forgiveness?

It is important to consider these factors, because what might be important to me – in terms of gaining an education and meeting my goals – may seem unimportant to someone else who is just trying to survive. As my father was required to quickly make money and support himself out of high school, he could not envision a world where education would take priority. This does not make him right and me wrong or vice versa, it simply lends insight. When we have insight, we can have mutual a understanding and respect.

One benefit my dad, and others who immediately enter the workforce after high school, have over those of us who pursued college degrees is years on the job. When you look for a job, the post will undoubtedly be requesting a specific number of years of experience. The problem is, how can you get the experience without a job in the first place? I have had this pull for a long time, to want to be more; to be older and more experienced. I have always struggled with defining experience, but not in the sense of how to use the word. I know that it is describing an instance or time that leaves an impact and shapes us. I know that many job descriptions list the years of experience desired. But I have always gotten caught on how much experience is enough. When I have done a job 5 years? 10 years? 50 years?

Maybe my problem is my focus on experience as an end goal, in terms of the quantitative number, rather than the overall impression. When I really sit back and think about it, the value of the experience is much greater than the quantity. I could sit in a position for 10 years without attempting to grow or do more than what is asked of me. Or I could take every opportunity to learn, explore different perspectives, remain insightful to how I interact with and impact people, for a much shorter period of time, and be all the more effective. Some may think that makes me entitled. Some may think if we bust our butts long enough, we have worked hard enough to deserve the promotion. Some may think that only the number of years will define your competence in providing leadership or knowing how to interact with the world. Value of experience is in the eye of the beholder, and also on which end of the quantity-quality spectrum of experience the beholder exists.

This is as true for experience as it is for education. I personally cannot get enough education. I love learning new things and believe knowledge is power. That is not to say that those who do not have education-based knowledge are powerless. Knowledge can come from both experience and education. If we accept that one person's dreams and goals are better supported by one or the other, and support them in that pursuit, we can band together in our knowledge and power and really get shit done.

Lazy and Hardworking

My mother's parents are in their eighties, and still working their farm. My grandfather has had a successful business of logging trees with draft horses. He has continued to do so over the years despite advances in large machines and tractors. He still maintains a farm with horses and other livestock. My grandmother maintains the home. She cooks three meals a day for my grandfather and any guests, such as farm hands, that may be visiting on any given day. My grandparents have been maintaining these hardworking roles together in their home for over 60 years. Their continuation to maintain their home and farm is what I see as good, old-fashioned hard work.

Our society and other developed countries around the world have become less dependent on agriculture and more dependent on processed foods, and have made advances in technology, science, and mental and physical healthcare. There has been a shift in what is defined as work. I can't say how many times I have seen or heard someone say, "you know what the problem with today's youth is? They just don't work hard enough." At the same time we are seeing an increasing trend of workaholics - people who, work not just more hours than the current standard, but feel internal pressures to work, have persistent thoughts about work when not working, and who work beyond what is reasonably expected of them, as established by the requirements of the job or basic economic needs, despite the potential for negative consequences (e.g., marital issues).[68]

In researching this topic, it seems it is not just me that sees workaholism as a controversial topic. After all, if you believe our current workforce is just not working hard enough, then you probably think of people who are working harder - obsessed with the idea of work and accomplishing more and more - as a positive thing.

The changes can be simplified. If the majority of the population is not living off the land, the majority of the population is not required to work 16-18 hour days in the fields and doing chores on the farm. I am one of those people who just has a run of the mill 8:00am to 5:00pm office job. I don't even have a window. I work in a seated position (with the option to stand at a raised desk), staring at a computer the majority of the day. I do not work a 16-hour day. I do not do physical labor. I am in

---

[68] Clark, M. (2016). Workaholism: It's not just long hours on the job. American Psychological Association. Retrieved from http://www.apa.org/science/about/psa/2016/04/workaholism.aspxz

the millennial generation. "Fuckin' millennials" as my husband would say. We still go back and forth before he admits that he is in the same generation. Our generation has gotten a bad rap and is drowning in stereotypical beliefs about how lazy and entitled we are.

I am not going to sit here and say I am not entitled. I have had some incredibly shameful moments in the past few years, in which I have started to acknowledge my own entitlement. I did not even really know what entitlement meant, only that I shouldn't be it.

When I was 14, I remember my mom taking me around local shops and restaurants to apply for summer jobs. The little, rural town where I grew up – and still now live – is a tourist town. Maximum population of 1,500 during the months October through April, and then Memorial Day hits and boom, 10,000 people are flowing in and out of our local streets. I walked out of one of the little shops and into my mom's car. I filled out the application right there in her car and we debated how to fill out one particular section. I clearly remember saying, "I am just going to put this because they should just like me and want to hire me for who I am." She responded, "No, you need to put your best self and attributes on that application, so they see what you are capable of." My hope is that her intention was not to teach me to be deceitful, but rather to be confident of my abilities and able to communicate them. How I have seen that translate into my adult years is a sense of entitlement and expectation that I have already done enough and deserve the job/relationship/thing. Sometimes I see it as confidence. The other thing I see is what I have now identified as the imposter syndrome.

The imposter syndrome is a psychological phenomenon in which the person experiencing it feels like a fraud.[69] It is not surprising that I would feel like a fraud, when I have been acting on this advice from my mom to never let others see my weaknesses, and to only show my strengths and how good I can be. It is said that individuals that have this experience often grew up in families in which achievements were valued. These individuals might who continue to achieve one thing after another and feel inadequate regardless. They might feel as though they will be found out at any point; that someone is going to call them out on not being perfect.

Perfectionism often goes hand in hand with the imposter syndrome. Perfectionism, I believed for many years, simply meant that a person wanted to be perfect. What the name does not imply at first glance, though, is that not only is the individual seeking perfection, but they also experience tremendous stress when anything less than perfectionism is achieved. And well, we are human, so perfection is not attainable. I have been told for over a decade that I have perfectionist tendencies and though I can identify in small moments what that looks like, just recently I started noticing how it affects my relationship with others and my work.

---

[69] Craig, L. (2018). Are you suffering from imposter syndrome? American Psychological Association. Retrieved from https://www.apa.org/science/about/psa/2018/09/imposter-syndrome

I love the way Andie Mitchell writes about perfectionism in her book "It Was Me All Along:"

> "When we were done drawing, I'd decide to throw my picture away, because it was never as good as his. Not even close. I couldn't bear to see my illustration next to his, not when he was perfect. Later, when I was alone, I'd place his picture on the table beside me and strive to recreate it on a new sheet of construction paper. I wanted to make mine as good. I wanted Dad to like it."[70]

Perfectionism is almost like an addiction to achieve more and more; to get more responsibilities; to get another promotion. It keeps us from celebrating our accomplishments. When I achieve things, it validates that I am doing something right and that I am worthy and I belong. Brené Brown, in her work on shame and vulnerability, proposes that perfectionism is simply a type of armor. She would say that acknowledging our shortcomings and vulnerability is the most powerful and healthy thing we can do.

Unfortunately, sometimes I still feel like a fraud. These senses of imposter syndrome also go hand in hand with entitlement. The sense of entitlement that is so greatly associated with the millennial generation, is coursing through my blood, basically unbeknownst to me. That sounds pretty darn stereotypical though, does it not?

I started working in 2014, immediately after I graduated

---

[70] Mitchell, A. (2015). It was me all along: A Memoir. New York, NY: Clarkson Potter.

from my master's program. I was honest in my interview that I was not looking to be a case manager, the position I was being hired for, for long. When I learned less than a year later that a position was opening up to become a part-time clinician, which included a raise, I immediately applied for it. Another year later, when another job opened up, one in a middle management position, I applied, and I got the job. I remember reading that job description and thinking, "um, did they write this about me?"

I was in that job a few days less than one month when my new boss came to me to tell me she was leaving the agency. I had barely developed a relationship with this woman, but when she said, "We need a new CAPS director, and there is no reason that can't be you," I took it to heart.

I scheduled a lunch with her boss to talk about the position. Then I applied. Partly because I was feeling worthy of the job, partly because I needed to have another achievement under my belt - fueled by my perfectionistic tendencies - and partly because my new boss told me I could do it. Let me just say in retrospect, that I did not know I was being entitled.

Remember when I started this all by saying that I have had some shameful realizations? This was one of them. From where I sat, why wouldn't I get the job? I did not get that job. And I applied for another director position after that, and I did not get that either. And that is okay because sometimes we have to put in more time before we are provided the opportunity to prove ourselves at a higher level. A third time I applied for a director position and did not get that one either. Try and fail, try and fail. I will continue to work this way because entitlement or not, reaching for goals keeps me moving forward.

My boss when I was first hired on ended up getting hired My boss from when I was first hired at the agency was eventually hired as my former boss's predecessor. I am okay with that. At first, I was afraid. When I had taken my new position, I was sent in and not really given all the historical information that would have affected the way in which I approached other departments. Unfortunately, my new/old/first boss was in another department, which thought I was coming in like a hammer. Because of this, I was afraid she would not go to bat for the team that I had started to blend with over the course of the previous couple months. I am happy to say she definitely went to bat – in fact she has bunted, and she hit home runs for our team. She also provided me with some insight that I try to return to when I am starting to feel entitled or anxious to get to the next step.

The advice I got was to perform and master the skills in my current position. Once that has been accomplished, then it would be natural to move on to another position. That reminds me of a quote that reads, "The flower doesn't dream of the bee. It blossoms and the bee comes."[71]

This has been for the most part an effective strategy for me, because it allows me to focus on learning what I

---

[71] Nepo, M. (2000). *The book of awakening*. Newburyport, MA: Red Wheel

need to learn, in my current position. I can say to myself: The bee wants the blooming flower, not the silk facsimile. The bee wants the real, deliciously pollen-filled flower that takes its time to bloom.

Having this perspective can reduce stress. And stress is a real bitch. That is not fair though, because not all stress is bad. Some researchers have identified the eustress, which is stress that is actually beneficial to the person experiencing it. The Yerkes-Dodson Law which shows the relationship between pressure (stress) and performance,[72] shows that there isn't just a positive - the more stress, the more productivity - or negative - the less stress, the less productivity - correlation between stress and productivity. Rather, there is a curve at which a moderate amount of stress produces the most productivity. Too little stress is associated with disinterest and inattention. Too much stress is associated with impaired performance because of anxiety.

I was pretty excited to put a label on this. I am kind of into that, I guess. When I say "into," I mean it is a tendency I have and I am trying to work on it because labels and stereotypes can often go hand in hand.

When I was a junior in college, the year after my mom died, I lived in an old Victorian home with five other women and two bathrooms. Six of us women, and two

---

[72] Yerkes, R., & Dodson, J. (1908). The relation of strength of stimulus to rapidity of habit-forming. *Journal of Comparative Neurology and Psychology*, 18(5). Doi: 10.1002/cne.p20180503

bathrooms. the same time as me and "two girls and one cup". We were all freshly 21 years of age, and we lived within walking distance of what we thought were some of the best bars. I had a lot of fun that year. I partied hard, blacked out and puking, 3 or 4, (or more) nights a week; I took 5 classes, the most credits I had taken throughout my college career. I participated in two honors clubs; I worked a part-time job. I kid you not, I 4-pointed the semester. I do not recall those stories as a way of bragging. I simply find it interesting, that I had so much on my plate that every minute had to be balanced and planned, down to the time scheduled for my gnarly hangovers. With everything I had going on, my stress was high and so was my productivity.

I would venture to say this curve looks different depending on the person you are applying it to. Maybe I require a higher level of stress to reach optimal performance. Maybe the amount of stress that is required for someone else's optimal performance is in my danger zone to be either under or overwhelmed.

Someone who likes to shit on us millennials might say this is just another excuse or reason for me to be lazy or to not work a 16-18-hour day. This is one of those situations in which I respectfully say, "no offense and fuck 'em." Having the information that can aid in improving performance and satisfaction, does not make me weak or lazy, it makes me a smart worker. Just because I have that information, does not mean my whole generation does. Just because I am still working on how not to be an entitled ass, does not mean everyone else from my generation is also working on it, or even aware of it when they behave in the same way.

Conversely, just because you are not in the millennial generation, does not mean you are not or have never been entitled in the past. To stereotype that "young adults today" are lazy does not mean that other people are not lazy too.

As with everything else, there are so many factors that go into making people the way they are, and so many ways a person can be. They are not just lazy or hardworking. We are all on a continuum with everything in between, and we move within the continuum depending on the day, who we are with, our circumstances, if we are hungry, tired, not stressed enough or overly stressed. Basically, this all just means we are human, and we are doing the best we can with the upbringing, experiences, and genes we are given.

To make a generalization on how a person is or isn't based on the generation in which they were born is simply stereotyping. I guess you could say I am entitled just because I am a Millennial, but then you are really the one to sound like an ass.

Despite what others might perceive as missteps so far in my professional career, I continue to keep moving in the direction I want. When I was a high schooler, I would tell my parents that I wanted a "house husband." I would be the one to provide for our family, and he would stay home with our children, cook, clean and care for the house. My husband and I both work full time, but I would say that we both contribute equally to our housework and child-rearing.

Some might say that is the feminist in me to demand such equal contribution, and that is true. We should not bat an eyelash at a stay-at-home dad any more than we should at a stay-at home-mom. . I have heard it said that we should be grateful for the feminist movement that allowed us women to work outside of the home, and I am personally appreciative. At the same time, just because women choose to be stay-at-home moms does not mean we should be calling them anti-feminist. If the woman wants to stay home, that is her right. It feels more like a shift in stigmatization, in which women who are "just stay-at-home moms" are now more stigmatized than women who work outside of the home. Frankly this stereotyping is just as harmful as not allowing women to work outside of the home in the first place.

Whether you want to work outside of the home or not – because honestly, we all know that staying home is still work – you should be able to do what you want without a generalization on what your choice means for our culture. A woman who stays home based on a mutual decision between her and her partner, is not an asshole working against the feminist movement. The people who judge or stereotype her are the assholes.

Pussies and Violence

I've gone back and forth on the title of this chapter because I hate the word *pussy*. I hate it so much that it makes me cringe when I read it, and I almost become physically ill when I write or say it. The word has great meaning to me though. In the town where I grew up, pussy was a word to describe the weak. Specifically, a man was a pussy if he was showing emotion or acting unmanly. In my world, those things were synonymous.

The word *pussy* also happened to be a buzzword around the time of the 2016 presidential election campaign, when it was revealed that President-elect Donald Trump had talked about grabbing a woman by her pussy. Many defended Trump by stating that it was nothing more than locker room talk, something which I am all too familiar with considering where I grew up. The story jump started a movement of pink pussy hats, rallies and marches where women and men stood up to say, "nope, can't say pussy like that, can't grab pussy like that, just nope."

Push-back also came out of this movement, as racial minority populations expressed their underrepresentation when a pussy was described as pink. I do not disagree with the argument and at the same time, understand that every movement cannot be inclusive of all populations. Responders to the criticism say the reference to pink was to destroy the gender stereotype color, pink, rather than the color of a pussy. Ultimately, one races' females are not less important than others, though they likely experience different types of discrimination and oppression. If we band together, we have a larger army... but I digress.

Equality is not just about women, either. Instead of teaching our sons to never hit a woman, how about not hitting anyone? How about respecting one another and treating one another kindly because we are all humans? Indicating one gender is more superior than the other, is harmful to all genders. In earlier chapters, we established how beneficial vulnerability can be to our mental health and stability. Unfortunately, vulnerability is still seen as a weakness and seeing vulnerability and weakness as a downfall is harmful to both men and women.

The American Psychological Association recently issued guidelines for practice with men and boys related to the pressures from toxic masculinity.[73] The main finding of research is that traditional masculinity—manifested by stoicism, competitiveness, dominance and aggression—is harmful. Men socialized in this way are less likely to engage in healthy behaviors such as preventative health care, accessing mental health services and eating vegetables, and more likely to engage in unhealthy behaviors such as heavy drinking and tobacco use.[74] It is believed that the societal expectations placed upon men to be tough, are contributing to higher proportion of men than women being offenders of violent crimes.

Unfortunately, instead of moving towards less violence, we are moving in the opposite direction. A report published by the Federal Bureau of Investigation (FBI) in 2015, studying active shooting situations - "a situation in which an individual actively engaged in killing or attempting to kill people in a confined and populated area" - defined between 2000 and 2013, found that these kinds of incidents are happening more and more. The first seven years of the study found an average of 6.4 active shootings per year, while the last seven years of the study found that number jumped up to 16.4 incidents

---

[73] Pappas, S. (2019). APA issues first-ever guidelines for practice with men and boys. *CE Corner, 50*(1). Retrieved from https://www.apa.org/monitor/2019/01/ce-corner

[74] Yousaf, O., Popat, A., & Hunter, M. S. (2015). An investigation of masculinity attitudes, gender, and attitudes toward psychological help-seeking. Psychology of Men & Masculinity, 16(2), 234-237. Retrieved from http://dx.doi.org/10.1037/a0036241

per year.[75] Since that time, shootings continue to occur.[76] The day after my second son was born, my husband and I watched in horror as a shooting at a country music concert in Las Vegas left 58 people dead and 546 injured. That shooting is categorized as an active shooting as described previously, and also meets the definition of a mass shooting – "episodes of three or more people are killed."[75] By August of 2019, 255 mass shootings had occurred during the calendar year.[77]

We live in a time where someone can walk into a school, unload an automatic weapon, and kill or injure dozens of innocent lives in the matter of minutes. It happens so frequently now that we are becoming desensitized. We are rarely surprised when another shooting hits the news. The country goes crazy trying to identify the cause. But rather than talking about a solution we try to point blame and talk about who is wrong.

The liberals are wrong because all they want to do is take away all the guns, leaving the citizens unprotected. The conservatives are wrong because they are putting

---

[75] Ehrenfreund, M. & Goldfarb, Z. A. (2015). 11 essential facts about guns and mass shootings in the United States. https://www.washingtonpost.com/news/wonk/wp/2015/06/18/11-essential-facts-about-guns-and-mass-shootings-in-the-united-states/?utm_term=.3d3f86815bfc

[76] Bonn, S.A. (2017) Mass public shootings are on the rise. Retrieved from https://www.psychologytoday.com/us/blog/wicked-deeds/201711/mass-public-shootings-are-the-rise

[77] Silverstein, J. (September 1, 2019). There have been more mass shootings than days this year. Retrieved from https://www.cbsnews.com/news/mass-shootings-2019-more-mass-shootings-than-days-so-far-this-year/

money and guns into the hands of dangerous criminals who will continue to engage in gun violence. On the one hand, the indirectly affected people who are responding with fear, grief, and sadness are a bunch of pussies and need to "man up." At the same time, the hardened and sociopathic comments and beliefs are what lead to acts of violence in the first place. These dichotomous and blaming opinions are a mess.

We as parents have a huge responsibility to raise decent human beings. I am honored, humbled and completely terrified of this responsibility. I frequently feel sadness that my parents were not around to watch me marry my husband, start and grow in my professional career, and grow and deliver two baby boys. I think they would be proud. This sadness spills into frequent thoughts of not having my own mother to validate my struggles as a mom of little ones, give me parenting ideas, and tell me, "I was there too, and you turned out just fine." I laugh to myself with both joy and sadness over the many times my mom told me, "I'm sorry, but you didn't come with a manual." Becoming a mother myself I am slowly learning the greatness of what she meant by that.

I became a parent willingly though acknowledge that not everyone does. Regardless of how someone becomes a parent, and regardless if it was wanted or unwanted, parents deserve support. Support can look a lot of different ways. I think primarily people turn right to abortion and begin the argument with murder and how insurance should not have to pay for it.

The lack of support I usually see goes further beyond

that. If you have ever seen the video of a high school gym class, in which the teacher has the students line up next to one another, but different people get to take multiple steps forward prior to racing one another, you may have some insight in to privilege. Essentially, they are standing in a line like in the kids' game Red Rover. Some of the children get to take steps forward by assignment based on their race, gender or socioeconomic status. The idea is to show how completely uncontrollable factors can put us ahead or behind to deal with situations life might throw at us. If an unwanted pregnancy results in the birth of a baby and the mother chooses to keep her child, where is the support at that point? If the mother is privileged in terms of growing up in a safer neighborhood, having two parents close by with college educations and stable jobs, having financial and emotional support, or having white skin, she will have far more resources available to her than a black mother with an absent father and little to no financial support despite the fact that her mother works three jobs trying to make ends meet.

Privilege is tricky, because there can be a certain level of stereotyping required to explain it. What we should remember is that privilege may cause one person to have fewer resources and as such, that person requires more support due to factors out of their control.

I am not even just referencing social services, insurance, and food stamps here. I think support comes from an emotional and non-judgmental place as well. How can we convey empathy and support to a mother who was recently visited by Child Protective Services, because her young children were left home alone in the middle of the night while she worked the graveyard shift? Is punishing her with mandated parenting classes - which take up more of her time and resources she doesn't have - really the way to support her and make life better for her and her children? Maybe, but I doubt it.

Honestly, I do not know the answer on how we can provide support. Maybe our support comes from the many small opportunities to choose kindness and love - rather than judgment and punishment - that combine to provide a safety net for those who need it. If that assistance lightens the load on the parents, perhaps it also lightens the load on the child. For an illustration of this, think of all the cliché movies that show the high school bully being bullied at home.

When I was younger, I used to ask my mom why people were so mean. She said, "people are mean because they are hurting on the inside." Unfortunately, at that time I thought it meant that we just had to accept that as part of the relationship. I now know we can acknowledge the causes for someone's behavior and still advocate for our own needs. If the person who needs advocating is a child, how can we respect the parent's circumstances and support the child?

When we do not get to the root of the problem, we see children who are bullied at home come to school and bully others. Bullying is a broad description of behavior that is intended to harm, intimidate, or coerce someone more vulnerable. The relationship between bullying and violence can be shown with a very fine and also blurry line. In one sense, bullying is a form of violence. Some argue that due to the nature of bullying - which can be emotional, verbal, physical, online, via text or in person - that it extends beyond violence, because violence is only physical. I would argue that violence can be physical, but it could expand beyond the physical because of its definition as behavior involving physical force or strength of emotion.[78] It is not a stretch to say that bullying, whether emotional or physical, contributes to the violence in this country. Whether someone harms themselves or harms others, we know for certain that they are hurting. This does not provide an excuse, but when we know the root cause, we can start to come up with solutions.

One population that is all too often named during these acts of violence are people who struggle with a mental illness. I always find it to be an overgeneralization when every shooter is described as mentally ill. I used the word hurting before, because although mental illness may be associated with some acts of violence, to assume it is associated with all acts of violence, usually makes people believe that mental illness and violence go hand in hand.

According to several studies, 60-75% of the general public believe violence and mental illness are related. While studies exploring the relationship show varying

---

[78] Merriam Webster Dictionary (2019). Violence. Retrieved from https://www.merriam-webster.com/dictionary/violence

results, it is likely much smaller than believed. Studies ultimately show that there are a multitude of factors that influence violent acts, including history of trauma, substance use and violent background.[79,80,81] Other research actually shows that individuals with a mental illness are 2.5 times more likely to be the victim than the perpetrator of violence. Studies show that somewhere around 10% of homicides are committed by people with a mental illness, as are only around 5% of overall violent crimes.[82] Like everything we have discussed thus far, to assume that someone who is violent must have a mental illness or vice versa, is to stereotype.

When it comes down to it, what we really need to know is that there is no one fix to violence. I do not believe there is one law or gun ban that will change the trajectory of the mass violence in this country. To compare or associate one race, gender or body part with violence or weakness is not just naive, but contradictory to the efforts required to make a change.

---

[79] Doheny, K. (2009). Mental illness and violence: A link? Retrieved from https://www.webmd.com/mental-health/news/20090202/mental-illness-and-violence-a-link#2

[80] Harvard Medical School (2011) Mental illness and violence. Retrieved from https://www.health.harvard.edu/newsletter_article/mental-illness-and-violence

[81] Canadian Mental Health Association – Durham (2019). The myth of violence and mental illness. Retrieved from https://cmhadurham.ca/finding-help/the-myth-of-violence-and-mental-illness/

[82] Swanson, J.W. & Holzer, C.E. (1991). Violence and ECA data. Letter. *Hospital and Community Psychiatry* 42, 954 955

I jokingly want to start a movement in which weakness is no longer associated with pussies, but rather with testes. At a dinner party one evening, I overheard my friend's father call someone a pussy. Feeling brave, I whipped my head around and said, "Let me tell you about pussies. Mine birthed two babies. Pussies can take a beating. When have your reproductive organs done something tougher than that?" It was quite an invigorating experience, even though he went on to state that his recent surgery was comparable to childbirth. Thinking back, I could have discussed the vulnerability of someone kicking him in his gems versus someone kicking me in the pussy, but it likely would not have made a difference.

Let's just not compare weakness to anyone's body parts. There is a whole slew of words called adjectives that could communicate exactly what we mean, instead of body shaming or stereotyping someone's gender.

Tiny Houses and Materialism

I have been in therapy on and off for over 15 years. In the past year, as I have dug into my upbringing and experiences that make me the way I am, I have had many of those 'ah-ha' moments. Ah-ha moments are the times when something finally clicks; when something finally makes sense, even if you have heard it a dozen times before. In one specific session, I had several ah-ha moments within 5 seconds, experiencing excitement, shock, enlightenment, and slight annoyance.

There I was with the therapist I had seen several times and suddenly, I realized where my impulsive spending and retail therapy comes from. I recalled some pretty painful memories sandwiched with how well off I was in many other ways. Holidays were always magical, Santa always brought dozens of presents, the Easter Bunny always delivered overflowing Easter baskets and birthdays were always special. This was an interesting realization for me because what I was saying was, "sure my dad yelled at me sometimes, sure I was told I was fat, or not good enough, or didn't do enough, but I sure did have pretty much everything I ever wanted." Earlier, I recalled a frequent topic of conversation I had with my mom as a kid in which she told me she was lucky to have one present on Christmas and that she was determined to make it more special for her kids.

Figuring out what makes us who we are can provide a sense of peace. It allows us to acknowledge that we are not inherently bad or good. Rather, there are a number of factors that contribute to who we are and how we can best respond. Once we know where something comes from, we can figure out how to fix it, how to change it, how to be better. As someone who is constantly trying to remind myself that my shit does not, in fact, smell like roses, it feels counterproductive to point out something that makes me realize that being the way I am is not entirely my fault. There is certainly some point of responsibility in what I am choosing to do as an adult. Maybe it is nice to know I am not just a selfish, intentionally malicious, shopaholic (insert shrug).

It is kind of a sad joke in my family that several of us, particularly women, engage in "retail therapy." It is not as though I don't realize that it is kind of messed up how much I like to get things. It is not even necessarily having the things, as much as getting them. A $5 t-shirt, a $1 pack of gum, a $40,000 car. The size of the purchase can certainly impact the level of high I experience, but I get a high either way.

My therapist responded with something so shocking that I am sure the metaphorical lightbulb over my head flashed at a level of brightness that could be seen in the next state over. She said, "because when you get things, you feel loved." Woah. If you have ever used shopping as a way to make yourself feel better and have never considered this as a possible cause, it is kind of ugly. I do not want to be someone who associates material things with love. At the same time, that is exactly what I have done subconsciously for the majority of my life and it is something I am starting to do with my children.

With every birthday, holiday and even trips to the store, I like to give my children the things. I can say with 100% certainty that it is not the only way I express love to my children. I hug them more times in one hour than I can count, I tell them I love them, I snuggle them and meet their basic needs without asking for anything in return. I am committed to raising kind and generous boys and that, in itself, feels like a way of showing love. When I think of those things, I realize the material things are not so important.

Unfortunately, we are in a time when everywhere we look, there is some marketing or advertisement telling us what we need. Advertisements use psychological patterns to appeal to us as consumers. They show us two people in love, holding hands and frolicking down the beach to show us that if we buy that laundry detergent/bathing suit/diet program/cologne/timeshare, that we too will be happy and loved.

Capitalism can be a great thing. I have recently started

preparing to pursue my Master of Business Administration and since I have spent my time up until now studying psychology and social work, I have started to dabble in some business basics before I start classes. When I explore these topics, my head spins off. Capitalism is what makes up the American Dream. The very reason we now have the largest gap between the richest and the poorest in our country is based on the ideal that we do not all get the same amount of money based on our jobs. If we did, Bill Gates and Steve Jobs likely would not have become the entrepreneurs they were, handing us technology-changing devices that you may be reading this book on right now.

Capitalism is an economic and political system in which a country's trade and industry is privatized for profit rather than controlled by the state. When I think of the word capitalism, I picture a man in a fancy suit working for a private insurance agency, ripping money out of people's pockets and making a profit on someone's sickness. It can certainly paint an ugly picture, and I have heard it referenced poorly by some of my closest family and friends. Capitalism creates inequality and allows monopolies.

The way things are bought and sold have both good and bad tenents. The truth is, each side has a benefit and consequence. The opposite of capitalism is communism. Communism is derived from a theory by Karl Marx, which describes a governmental and economic system in which all wealth is equally distributed. Rather than individuals owning land, property, and business, the government does. When I think of communism, I don't necessarily jump for joy. The opposite of communism is democracy because democracy gives voice to the people, rather than to a reigning government. We cannot have democracy without capitalism. So yes, we choose to live in a free world, which means there is a large discrepancy between the richest and the poorest. It means we have a ridiculous wealth gap.

According to a 2016 survey done by the Federal Reserve, our country's wealth distribution and inequality continues to increase.[83] It is not as though the rich are getting richer and the poor getting poorer. We are in fact, all getting richer in the sense that the average household income is increasing overtime. However, the rich are holding more of the nation's wealth compared to the poor. As of 2016, the top 1% held 38.6% of the nation's wealth, up from 33.7% in 2007. The bottom 90% held 22.8% of the nation's total wealth, down from 28.5% in 2007. Basically, we have one pie and the rich keep getting a bigger slice.

This disparity varies based on race as well. The wealth gap is larger for white folks than it is for black.[84] One might assume this is because minority populations have less opportunity than their white counterparts. Even if the wealth gap does exist for minority populations, they

---

[83] Board of Governors of the Federal Reserve System. (2016). Survey of Consumer Finances (SCF). Retrieved from https://www.federalreserve.gov/econres/scfindex.htm

[84] McKernan, M.S., et al. (2015). Nine charts about wealth inequality in America. Retrieved from http://apps.urban.org/features/wealth-inequality-charts/

are being limited to an overall lower amount of wealth. This in itself is an issue of inequality and tilts the pendulum in the direction of communism.

Some argue that capitalism is the root cause of materialism. If capitalism is the free trade of goods and services to earn a profit, then the individuals attempting to earn a profit are going to try to sell said goods and services. Companies' efforts at advertising and marketing to sell us material goods often means we become obsessed with owning goods. When we place a higher value on owning goods than we do on spiritual or moral needs, we are living in a materialistic reality.

Here is the thing. Like everything else we have explored thus far, materialism is on a continuum. The value that we place on owning this or is are greatly varied and based on numerous factors. The car we drive may be more important to us than the house we live in. Or the college we attend may be more important to us than the clothes we wear. The problem with materialism is not necessarily in how we place value on the materialistic things that we possess, but rather how we place a higher value on those things than we do on someone else's basic needs.

I do not think anyone likes taxes to be taken out of their paycheck. I certainly do not like the feeling that something I have worked for is taken from me without my consent. In the same breath, do I really need the extra five hundred bucks to buy that pair of Toms shoes or new Ray Bans? Not really. And especially not if that means it is taking those dollars out of a social program that helps a kid get access to food or housing. In this moment, I am proud to say that although getting things does make me feel good, it does not make me feel better than I do knowing we have a program that can help less fortunate people meet their basic needs.

I am not saying that government programs are perfect. Far from it. In addition to social programs, taxes go to both roads and corporate bailouts. They provide tax cuts for large corporations whose chief executive officers are making millions. Because of this, I know that my enemy is not someone who is in need but the budget line items making rich people richer.

I also work in a governmentally-funded agency, and have been privy to information in other governmentally-funded agencies that makes me question whether tax dollars are really going to people in need. The thing about capitalism is that there is little to no governmental regulation. The problem with governmental programs is that there is so much oversight. We waste money on things like attending meetings, so we can build relationships to ensure we get money for future programs and administrative staff to complete reporting and make sure we are in compliance. Those things take away from putting the money where it really needs to go: to the people.

We are in a broken system. While the difference between the rich and the poor is substantial, we now have people obsessed with tiny houses and Marie Kondo's decluttering techniques. My guess is, these are not the people in the richest two percent, as throwing out something that you might have to buy again when needed in six months is not a liberty afforded to poor people. The folks with the tiny houses may be the same people who believe in more equal distribution of wealth, but tiny houses are built and sold in free trade. If the government were responsible for the development of the tiny house movement, we would still likely be looking at another 20 years before they were even available because of the bureaucratic bullshit that is our government processes.

I am not saying definitively that capitalism is the way to go nor do I think an entirely government-run system is without shortcomings. What I am saying is we need to take the pieces that work and discard the rest, regardless of what it is called. What if I like both yoga and shopping profusely to find my center? Maybe I compost and use plastic baggies that very clearly harm our earth. What if I believe in God and evolution? I fight my dad's pack-ratty-ness and my mom's desire to have things to feel loved. I like all the things, and I am aware that I need to stop with all the things. This is something both very personal to me, and something much larger than me. My understanding of paying taxes to support someone who needs their basic needs met cannot change the world. My hope is to continually work towards fewer people living in poverty and suffering, even if that means I don't ever get to own a million-dollar mansion or a vacation home in Bora Bora.

Sexual Abuse and Crying Rape

When my mother died, I did all sorts of things to try to ease my pain, including controlling anything I could. I drank until I threw up in bushes - though this was more numbing than control - I slept with men without any sort of commitment (*I'm so cool I don't even need you to be my boyfriend*), and I counted my calories going in and being expended to the point of obsession. The year before my mom died however, I found God.

I can't remember how it happened. One day I was sleeping with a guy across the hall in my co-ed dorm, and the next I was attending services at a mega church once, twice and sometimes three times a week. If you have not caught on by now, I am a person who is compulsive in all sorts of behaviors, and churchgoing became my thing. I remember telling fellow churchgoers my story and explaining how I was baptized Methodist, raised in a Lutheran Church and had now found the love of Jesus Christ in the nondenominational church. It became my party line. I had church friends. I went to bible studies. I went on mission trips where we sang worship songs, prayed

together and encouraged others there to find Jesus themselves. I am so grateful for that time in my life because it helped make me who I am today. I met some wonderful people. It helped me question existence and contemplate the meaning of my dad's illness. It is also a great example of how I continue to live my life in periods of one obsession after another with an all-or-nothing view.

The spring before my mother died, I went on a mission trip to New Mexico. I was at the height of my church-going compulsion. The trip was nothing short of spectacular. I had so much fun, saw gorgeous mountainsides, met many wonderful people, and shared laughs and my heart. During the trip we were encouraged to share our stories. I remember sitting in a circle sobbing my eyes out over how difficult it was watching my dad's illness progress. I had no idea in just over a year; my mother would also die.

During this time, I decided to reclaim my virginity. I had spoken with some of my fellow Jesus lovers, and it was agreed upon by all that through prayer, I could make it a reality.

Up until this point, I was comfortable with my sexuality.

My mother was very open about reproductive health from a young age. My grandmother loved to tell a story about me, that when I was about four or five years old I held out a peach to her and said, "Look Grandma, it looks like a 'bagina'." I took five consecutive years of sex-ed and by the last year was correcting the teacher on vocabulary of the lady bits. My parents were very clear that abstinence until marriage was expected. That in its own way set a precedent that sex was shameful and dirty, as opposed to natural and loving, particularly once you are in a committed relationship. At the same time, I was not deprived of information on how to prevent diseases and pregnancy. I lost my virginity in high school. I never made it to a time in my life where I was able to talk openly about my sex life with my mother, but could envision open communication had she lived past my 19th year.

My sexual experiences were not lacking, but I still wanted a fresh start. I remember discussing reclaiming my virginity with someone and them saying, "you know that's not real right?" I politely - hopefully - disagreed. I decided that I could make whatever I wanted to be my reality. So, I did. It wasn't much of a challenge. I was spending time with other people who were also abstinent until marriage.

The first summer after reclaiming my virginity was a fun one. I was managing a small diner that served breakfast and lunch where I mostly hung out with a bunch of friends, 6 days a week. When I was not working, I worked out a couple of hours a day and slept the remainder of the time. A couple of times, I cruised around town with a couple girlfriends, blaring the hot new music of that time, and drinking vodka and crystal lite out of water bottles. For the most part, that summer involved working and working out. However, I also met a man.

I met the guy at my job. He was attractive and fun. He would join us on the beach, and we would make out in the bushes. I had expressed to him that I had reclaimed my virginity and that it was complicated. My college life of church-going and my home life of partying on the beach were completely paradoxical and that made it tough to get them to co-exist with limited cognitive dissonance. We dated for several months and, in the beginning, he was respectful of my decision to abstain from sex until marriage.

That year for Christmas, he came to visit me in my hometown. One of the nights we were partying at the cabin at which he was staying, and we snuck into the bedroom to fool around. Until this point, I had stuck with my commitment of abstinence. He said he had a gift to give me and I was skeptical. We were in the bedroom after all. He pulled out a pink vibrating sex toy. I was okay with it, because it didn't necessarily mean we had to have sex, right? Unfortunately, he had something else in mind. As we continued fooling around, he started trying to get on top of me. I didn't want to have sex, and I said so to him. He persisted though, and so I gave in. I cried the whole time and he didn't stop.

I look back on the experience and realize it is not a

brutal rape. He did not beat me, and he was my boyfriend after all. But when I recall the memory, I feel slightly sick and dizzy. I was sad, and it was not something I wanted. I look back on it and think, “why didn’t he stop? Why wouldn’t he have seen my tears and stopped to make sure I was okay?”

I am not sure if I shared this experience with anyone right away. Years later, I was talking with someone about sexual experiences and force. I am a complex person who both shares too much and is highly guarded. Finding balance about who deserves to hear my story is challenging for me as I tend to wear my heart on my sleeve. At other times, I minimize experiences and feelings and therefore don’t share at all. This experience though, I did share. I said I did not want to have sex with him and that I cried, and it was a difficult memory for me. In this instance, I was showing genuine vulnerability with someone I felt was safe. Their response was, “but you weren’t really raped.” And my answer was, “no, I guess I wasn’t.”

I want to be clear. I am not by any means saying that as some young white woman having semi-consensual sex is as devastating as incest, ongoing sexual assault and/or abuse, or violent rapes. If this book is anything, it is trying not to compare my experiences to somebody else’s, but rather acknowledge them exactly as they are. The point is that each of our experiences are just as they are; nothing more, nothing less. Regardless of the severity, experiences that cause pain are worthy of respect and empathy. Rather than comparing our experiences to one another's, we should be sitting with the discomfort together, acknowledging each other's pain exactly as it is, respecting each other's experience and accepting each other where we are.

The year after my mom died, I started hooking up, noncommittally with another guy. We did not go on dates or spend time together in public. We would meet up whenever our parents were not around - usually at his house - hook up and I would leave. He was pretty rough and at the time, I liked it. I was hurting inside after losing my mom and perhaps that was a way to have my physical experience equal my emotional pain. I remember one afternoon in which he was being so rough, to the point I was actually crying. He was choking me and had my face in a pillow. He was saying how much I liked it and I was thinking, "no not really" but did not find the nerve to say it to him out loud. Maybe I even asked for it. Of course, if another woman told me that story, I would validate the thought but remind her that he also had responsibility to communicate and make sure that she felt safe.

Fortunately, shortly after this I ended up meeting another guy that I got into a monogamous relationship with, and had to end it with the other guy. I remember telling him, "I met someone and think there might be something there so I can't see you anymore." Nobody likes rejection, and he was no exception. I cannot remember the full extent of the things he said to me, but he said more than once that I was "disgusting" and that "nobody would want me anyway." I told him once that if he said it again that I would stop speaking to him all together. We had gone to school together and we had many common friends, so attempting to remain civil was the goal. He stopped for a little while. We never had a relationship, so surely, we could remain friends, right? Wrong. A couple weeks later he continued with his hateful words of how gross of a human being I was; saying many things to make me feel belittled and worthless. At that point, I stopped talking to him. I blocked him from all forms of communication, and I have not spoken with him in over a decade.

I had forgotten many details about my time with that guy until my husband and I were talking about some sex thing that I never let him try. I had a flashback to that time with that guy so many years ago. I had not realized until that point how much it affected me. It had nothing to do with my husband or the specific type of sex at all. It had everything to do with the hateful words that some man told me after doing just the sex act that my husband was talking about.

We hear it a lot: "she put herself in that position" or "she was asking for it." Maybe I did, but did I deserve to be told such terrible things? Did I deserve to be put down and belittled because some guy was feeling rejected? Did I deserve to, for years, associate a type of sex with such a traumatic relationship?

How often have you heard someone blame the victim? "Did you see what she was wearing?" I don't care what you wear; I don't care if you run around in lingerie or butt ass naked, every human being deserves respect and respect means not being forced, raped, abused, or mistreated. It means if someone looks in distress, we ask if they are okay. Period. What if it was your mother, sister, brother, or best friend? Would you still make the same assumption?

I have talked a lot about cognitive biases throughout this book, because these psychological phenomena speak to how we develop certain beliefs and perspectives. Optimism bias leads you to believe that you are less likely to suffer from misfortune and more likely to attain success than your peers. It has been hypothesized that this bias is evident in cultures around the world.[85]

Perhaps this is why people are able to look at victims of abuse and harassment with such judgment. We believe that it cannot happen to us or someone close to us. I am aware that my experiences are not nearly as violent as they could have been. However, they are my experiences, and they did have an impact on the way I feel about sex. They made me afraid, and they influenced the way I felt about certain situations and about myself. We looked at the definition of violence earlier in the book: behavior involving physical force or strength of emotion. All things considered, that is enough for it to be called sexual violence.

We picture rape as the one violent act in which a stranger follows a woman down a dark alley, beats her profusely, rips her underwear and rapes her violently.

---

[85] Sharot, Tali. (2012). The optimism bias. Retrieved from https://www.ted.com/talks/tali_sharot_the_optimism_bias

We may even picture a step-father, uncle or older brother sneaking into a young girl's room at night and playing a "game." We know though, that these situations are not representative of all types of sexual violence. We know that rape is the most under-reported crime, in which only 37% are predicted to be reported to police and that as little as 12% of child sexual abuse cases are reported to the authorities. We also know that available data suggest that in some countries, nearly one in four women may experience sexual violence by an intimate partner.[86, 87,88]

We have these stereotypical views of what rape and sexual assault look like, and it is not truly representative of the problem. What about men? Men represent 9% of the population who have experienced rape and sexual assault. While the number may be far less than the 91% that encompasses female victims, it does not make their

---

[86] Rennison, C. M. (2002). Rape and sexual assault: Reporting to police and medical attention, 1992-2000 [NCJ 194530]. Retrieved from the U.S. Department of Justice, Office of Justice Programs, Bureau of Justice Statistics: https://www.bjs.gov/content/pub/pdf/rsarp00.pdf

[87] Hanson, R. F., Resnick, H. S., Saunders, B. E., Kilpatrick, D. G., & Best, C. (1999). Factors related to the reporting of childhood rape. *Child Abuse and Neglect*, 23(6), 559-569.

[88] World Health Organization. (2014). World Report on Violence and Health. Retrieved from
http://www.who.int/violence_injury_prevention/violence/global_campaign/en/chap6.pdf

experiences any less traumatizing or any less real.[89]

What about the drunken college girl who is raped at a fraternity house, and nobody believes her because she was drunk? More than 90% of sexual assault victims on college campuses do not report the assault, while the prevalence of false reporting of rape is between 2 and 10%. And yet, victim-blaming is rampant.

"She was asking for it" has become a frequent response to reports of sexual assault. The phrase "crying rape" is something that is accepted as a norm. The truth is there is a nearly imperceptible number of cases that are false, and a much larger number of cases which are never reported in the first place. Our preconceived notion that something needs to fit within our definition of sexual assault or rape in order to be considered "real rape," is what contributes to the sexual violence that continues in our culture.

Because of the prevalence at which women are the victims of sexual violence, we often forget who all it impacts. When I was in college, I worked at a non-profit organization called Women At Risk, International (WAR) in southwest Michigan. I was pulled on board as a marketing and sales assistant, which was a bit out of my wheelhouse. However, it provided me the opportunity to learn more about the ongoing world of human

---

[89] The United Nations. (2016). Report: Majority of trafficking victims are women and girls; one-third children. Retrieved from https://www.un.org/sustainabledevelopment/blog/2016/12/report-majority-of-trafficking-victims-are-women-and-girls-one-third-children

trafficking.

WAR partners with places around the world to complete outreach, provide safe and fair employment opportunities through microbusiness, and host safehouses both internationally and domestically. I cannot say I agree with all of the outreach efforts, because I worry they may look like Jehovah's Witness tactics. One of the programs occurring domestically was to visit the dancers at strip clubs and offer them a different life. Perhaps it is my own prejudices, but I feel those women likely have more freedom than a woman who is drugged and locked in a whorehouse in the red-light district. That could also be that black-and-white thinking we have explored so much thus far. Regardless, what I have been trying to convey throughout this whole book is that everyone should have the right to do what they want as long as they are not hurting themselves or others.

A common misconception of WAR, likely due to the deceiving organizational name, is that they are only helping women and girls. They support men too. Sexual violence and human trafficking are not exclusive to women. Because the victims are majority female, it is easy to stereotype who we think of as victims and perpetrators. A 2016 report by the United Nations showed that 51% of victims were women, 21% men, 20% girls, and 8% boys. This same source reports, "trafficking for sexual exploitation and for forced labor remain the most prominently detected forms, but victims are also being trafficked to be used as beggars, for forced or sham marriages, benefit fraud, or production of pornography."[90]

Human trafficking shows even more of a variance in who is affected. The National Sexual Violence Resource Center reports 91% of rapes and sexual assault victims are women while 9% are men. Despite the vast population representation, there is no benefit to minimizing the impact of violence on non-female victims. Sexual violence can lead to any combination of issues, including but not limited to depression, flashbacks, post-traumatic stress disorder, self-harming behaviors, sexually transmitted infections, substance abuse, eating disorders, sleep disorders and suicide. Men are no less vulnerable to these effects solely because of their gender. In fact, that would wildly contradict the point I am trying to make. In addition to the aforementioned impact, men and boys may have a more unique set of responses based on social attitudes and stereotypes about men and masculinity.[91]

Our genders do not give us benefits or consequences in and of themselves. The social constructs that created what it means to be male and female are what harm us. The beauty of this is that we have the opportunity to change social constructs. We have the opportunity to

---

[90] National Sexual violence Resources Center. (2015). Statistics about sexual violence. Retrieved from https://www.nsvrc.org/sites/default/files/publications_nsvrc_factsheet_media-packet_statistics-about-sexual-violence_0.pdf

[91] Rainn. (2019). Sexual assault of men and boys. Retrieved from https://www.rainn.org/articles/sexual-assault-men-and-boys

look at how our scoffing at others' experiences - whether male or female, rape or sexual assault, better or worse than our experiences - has an impact on the overall social construct. That puts the power back in our hands.

If we want to live in a world that moves beyond the stereotypes, prejudices, expectations and limitations - if we want to be respected, heard and understood - then we have to start accepting that the multiple levels and differences of someone else's experience are just as real as our own. It is not less, it is not more, it just is.

Conservatives and Liberals

Like many other opposing beliefs my parents had, my mother identified as a Democrat and my father as a Republican. I remember my mom telling me they stopped voting early in their marriage because their votes seemed to always just cancel each other out. During the 2008 election, I remember my mom telling me how much she enjoyed listening to Barack Obama deliver his speeches, and my dad would follow with discord because he knew that any Democrat elected would just take all our guns away.

Since the first election I was able to participate in, I have noticed our country becoming increasingly characterized by ideological polarization between Democrats and Republicans. It is likely that this phenomenon has far predated my voting history. In fact, some studies show an increase in polarization over the past 25 years. Since 1994, the number of Americans who are unvaryingly liberal or conservative has doubled. Additionally, it's been found that the typical Republican is now more conservative than 94% of Democrats and the typical Democrat is now more liberal than 92% of Republicans.[92]

It has been proposed that the parties' platforms are based on ten issues: government efficiency, governmental regulation of businesses, social programs and support, racial equality, immigration, how to ensure peace, corporation policy, environmental regulation, and LGBTQ rights.[93] Maybe it is just me, but I do not fit in a nice box based on these ten items. Yet each election, I am forced to choose either a Republican or a Democrat to represent me.

Based on the lack of verbiage in the United States Constitution on political parties, one might assume that the founding fathers did not intend for politics to be partisan. Our first president, George Washington, did not identify with a political party. In his farewell address, he solicited the absence of political parties for fear of conflict and inertia in politics.

In the 1700s the first party system was developed, which included the Federalist party and the Democratic-

---

[92] Pew Research Center: U.S. Politics & Policy. (June 12, 2014). Political polarization in the American public: How increasing ideological uniformity and partisan antipathy affects politics, compromise and everyday life. Retrieved from https://www.pewresearch.org/topics/political-polarization/

[93] US History.org (2019). American political attitudes and participation: What factors shape political attitudes. Retrieved from http://www.ushistory.org/gov/4b.asp

Republican party. In 1828, the Democratic and Republican parties split. During the earlier days, each party had significant overlap in their beliefs regarding tax policy, social programs and issues, labor and free trade, health care, foreign policy, environmental concerns, education, crime and capital punishment, and individual liberties. Over time, the parties have polarized to have less overlap in the way they vote and in the beliefs they represent.

Group polarization is defined in psychology as when discussion leads a group to adopt attitudes or actions that are more extreme than the initial attitudes or actions of the individual group members.[94] Have you ever considered how your political beliefs came about? I am certain there are thousands of factors. Research has shown genetics account for 30-60% of variance in political beliefs.[95] I would also venture that the party with which you associate guides you towards what to believe as well.

Political parties have become so polarized that we now see two completely opposing parties, rather than a continuum of beliefs which likely more accurately describes our country's political makeup. I have to frequently remind myself that someone who has

---

[94] Brauer, M., Judd, C. M., & Gliner, M. D. (1995). The effects of repeated expressions on attitude polarization during group discussions. *Journal of Personality and Social Psychology*, 68, 1014-1029.

[95] Hatemi, P.K., et al. (2014). Genetic influences on political ideologies: Twin analyses of 19 measures of political ideologies from five democracies and genome-wide findings from three populations. *Journal of Behavioral Genetics*, 44(3): 282-294.

different beliefs than me does not necessarily care about equality or the children impacted by our current immigration wars; it is more likely that they believe in prioritizing money and efforts towards another cause that they support.

Politics are all about money now, and I think that is something we can certainly all agree on. The problem is that we are stereotyping one another as our political positions polarize, and are starting to see each other as the outgroup, as the enemy. When we see each other as not belonging to our same group, we are more likely to stereotype and hate them.[96]

Studies have shown that we are at a point where we make assumptions about one another just based on the political party with which we associate. According to the study by Pew Research Center, 38% of Democrats and 43% of Republicans now view the opposite party in strongly negative terms, and 36% of Republicans say Democratic policies threaten the nation whereas 27% of Democrats say the same about Republican policies.[97]

If we would just stop for a minute and look at what is really happening, we would all be able to see that neither party benefits when they work against one another. It is the politicians who benefit. It is not the middle and

---

[96] Allport, G.W. (1954). *The nature of prejudice.* Cambridge, MA: Addison-Wesley.

[97] Pew Research Center: U.S. Politics & Policy. (2014). Political polarization in the American public: How increasing ideological uniformity and partisan antipathy affects politics, compromise and everyday life. Retrieved from https://www.people-press.org/2014/06/12/political-polarization-in-the-american-public.

upper working-class folks who are hoping for lower taxes. And it is certainly not the lower-class folks who are barely making ends meet. It is the large corporations receiving governmental bailouts and still earning massive profits, because they are lining the pockets of the politicians who we keep voting in. Our politicians are no longer representing us. It has been said that prior to his election that President Donald Trump was associated with the Democratic party, but when he decided to run, he ran as a Republican because he had a higher chance of winning. That is not someone who is doing due diligence to represent their constituents, as is intended.

One piece of advice I will always remember is, "never discuss two things while drinking: religion and politics." Sadly, this happens more often than I would like. It is often just hurtful, and unsurprisingly, I have yet to be swayed or to sway the other person to change beliefs. The best we can do is try to come together in compromise, to meet the most needs possible. This can only happen if we have conversations with people who do not believe in everything that we do, we treat others with respect, and we ask questions. I firmly believe that the neediest folks are not the politicians or the corporations, but the average Americans.

Thankfully, we have seen political parties change throughout history, and so our best hope to achieve true representation is to see a change within political parties. It is simply not enough to be confined to one side or another.

A few years ago, a family member asked me to

participate in a survey regarding political beliefs; left versus right. The survey contained questions you would expect, including beliefs surrounding gun rights, abortion, immigration, education, and taxation. I always feel the need to explain myself when these topics come up. If you could not tell by now, I am primarily liberal in my beliefs. But I was also raised in a small rural town in the Midwest where I started shooting guns and eating meat hunted by my dad at a young age.

I am rarely fully represented by either party due to my belief in the right to bear arms. The liberal in me certainly comes out a bit when I start asking for increased background checks, but in due course, I do not want to see my guns taken away either. Honestly, I believe both parties are right and wrong in some respects. Of course, right and wrong are completely subjective. I can say with certainty that I believe politicians have their own interests in mind, more often than not, and therefore are not truly able to represent me either way.

Participating in that survey lead me to describe my political beliefs as the right for people to have their rights and opinions. Whatever we are doing right now is not working - our prisons are full, our mental health systems are failing, our education systems are totally funky, and way too many people are dying of drug overdoses. I think that is something we can all agree on, regardless of our chosen political party.

Feminism and Femininity

When I first started dreaming up the idea of this book, approximately ten years prior to writing it, I knew I would call it *Feminist in Pink*. I grew up in a small, rural town in which hunting and fishing were done both as a sport and for the provision of food throughout the year. I was born in the middle of one sister and one brother and felt for a long time that I was constantly going from girly things with my mom to not-so-girly things with my dad.

I remember my mom laughing at me one day when I spent the morning with her and my sister painting our nails then headed out back with my dad and brother to shoot guns. If you remember from a few chapters back, one of the only ways I saw to connect with my dad was to go hunting with him. I cried a lot when I shot things and I have had no interest in shooting anything since my trip with him out west. My husband is an avid hunter and a full-time fishing guide, and even he can't talk me into getting back out in the "great outdoors" to hunt. Despite this, I do love to shoot some guns. I like the feel of the gun when it kicks back after pulling the trigger. I like the smell of the gun powder. I like knowing I could protect myself and my family if I needed to. Knowing I would never go out of my way to intentionally harm someone or something, my love for guns is probably a power thing.

I was constantly getting contradictory lessons from my parents about what it means to be a woman. My parents told me I could be anything I wanted to be and at the same time, I observed my mom being the caretaker, staying at home with me and my siblings, cooking and cleaning; the stereotypical "mom" things. My dad was the breadwinner; running his own business and working what seemed like 20 hours a day. I do not remember him taking me to doctor's appointments, taking care of us when we were sick, or cleaning anything in the house. Mind you, I have heard from people outside of the family that mom had her hands in the business as well. This only confirmed my beliefs that women are expected to do everything and to do it all well. It is important to acknowledge what we are told, what we observe, what we experience, and understand how those things shape us. If we acknowledge it, we can question the source and the legitimacy of the thought or idea.

It is time we talk about stereotypes. A feminist in pink is an effort to break a stereotype. I pride myself on being open-minded. In being honest that I am unfamiliar with different cultures, whether it be in a different part of the world or a different socioeconomic status of someone down the road. In entering conversations with the ability to try to see things from another point of view. It was not until writing this book that I made the connection that my idea of a feminist in pink is about breaking a stereotype; that black-and-white thinking can lead to or is symbolic of stereotypes. Of course, I can be a feminist who likes the color pink and wears makeup.

Feminism is not about how a person looks anyway. In fact, if we wanted to get to the meaning of the word feminism, we would find that the equality that is being sought by feminists is in complete support of women being able to do whatever the hell they want exactly because they are women, not in spite of it. This is true regardless of the type of feminism we are talking about: liberal, radical, cultural, or intersectional. Frankly, I am not even sure what type of feminist you would define me as. I love the intersectional feminism framework created to explain how the feminist movement can be more diverse and inclusive. It accounts for the multiple overlapping identities such as race, class, ethnicity, religion and sexual orientation, and how those factors impact the way women experience oppression and discrimination.[98] I guess if you wanted to call me something I would love to identify as an intersectional feminist, but if you have yet to figure it out, I am not a fan of being limited by one category or another.

[98] Womenlite. (2019) What is intersectional feminism? Why is it important today? Retrieved from https://womenlite.com/intersectional-feminism/

The stereotypes about what a feminist looks like can get pretty old. My husband has often started stories about me by saying, "well Brenna's a huge feminist" as if by saying that, he explained all they needed to know about me. Some people just nod, some people say, "okay me too," and some purse their lips knowing what he is trying to convey. It is almost as if he is waiting for them to blow off his story if he starts it like that. I mostly just stand there nodding, my head tilted to the side like a dog waiting to be taken outside, wondering what story he is going to tell. It usually leads to a story about why I got upset about a news story or after witnessing some unjust situation. I am proud to be a feminist and I am praying to all the higher powers that my sons are too. My husband and I have actually spoken several times about how he, too, is a feminist in the true sense of the word. I just want everyone to be treated equally regardless of gender – or sexuality, race, ethnicity, or beliefs.

Our preconceived notions of what a feminist must sound, act, dress, or look like are all wrong. Our society makes it seem that if you are a man and a feminist, that you are betraying your gender. When equality for all genders is sought, it is not just women that benefit. That men must be strong and emotionless or be thought of as weak, is a social construct that could and should be destroyed. Constructs about what it means to be a man are completely detrimental to men and women alike. To associate any gender with any certain characteristic is part of the problem. It is cool by me if you want to lift weights and have biceps bigger than your head and that stands true if you are male or female. If you want to participate in peaceful marches to build awareness for equality for both sexes, that is cool too.

My beliefs and opinions do not make me better or worse than other humans. They just are what they are. When my beliefs or opinions translate to actions that hurt even one person, we have a problem. We are entitled to our beliefs and opinions; we are not entitled to harm others with our beliefs and opinions or violate someone else's human rights.

During the writing of this book, Donald Trump was elected president, and what a controversial time it was. I do not want to get too far into the politics of it all, as that is another whole book in itself. When I think of Donald Trump, I pretty much think anti-feminist. Throughout the election and basically every day after, the country (okay, world) talked about a story of Trump grabbing a woman "by the pussy" essentially because he could, even if she did not want it.

I am not saying I endorse that. I mean, obviously - have you been reading this book? What I am saying is just because someone says that they voted for Trump, does not mean they cannot believe in equal rights for women. Sure, they may overlook his gross behavior, but we all make decisions about what is important to us and allow some behaviors to slide for what we believe is for the greater good. The next time I think to myself, "You can't be a feminist! You support Trump!" I am going to try to challenge myself. I am going to consider the variations of beliefs and morals for people who also believe in equal rights for women. I do not want my feminist beliefs to be put into a box, so I should probably do the same for others. Golden rule and all, right?

The only way we can treat others as we would want to be treated is to listen. It can be incredibly challenging to take others' perspectives; to see their point or understand the experiences that have made them who they are.

During the summer before I went into 9th grade, my breasts grew from an A cup to a C-D cup within months. As a 14-year-old, I had yet to develop curves in any other part of my body, and many people would comment on how I had the "ideal body shape" with my big boobs and tiny waist. I have grown up struggling with body image and confidence, likely due to watching my mom do the same, so the feedback at the time felt positive. As I grew older, the weight of my chest became painful. Throughout high school and college, I maintained a weight in the low hundreds, but my breasts were in the DD range.

I said for many years that I would get a breast reduction someday. After I had children, my problem grew substantially. I struggled with muscle spasms in my back, neck, and shoulders, had frequent headaches and in one particular instance had terrible blisters on my rib cage from trying to find a well-fitting bra. I am by no means a professional athlete, but I enjoy staying active and participating in higher intensity workouts. Because I started researching the procedure early, I knew that it posed a risk of not being able to breastfeed, so I waited until I was done having children to pursue the surgery.

After I had my second son, I got very serious about exploring a provider. I had heard of a board-certified plastic surgeon in the area and saw his rave reviews. I set up an appointment for a consult and was pleasantly surprised at how quickly the consult and surgery were scheduled. I was impressed by the doctor's claim of having performed hundreds of breast reduction surgeries, and felt comfortable in his care. After the surgery, I was incredibly dissatisfied by the reduction. He was insistent that he had provided me the care that I had requested and noted how lifted my breasts were. I indicated to him that my overall goal was not to have a lift, but to be comfortable and symptom-free. I asked his office to send me my records of consultation and surgery. To my unpleasant surprise, the records in my chart documented an experience much different than my perspective.

During our first consult, he indicated droopy breasts as my first complaint, which was not the case. I indicated my chief complaints as daily headaches, back pain, neck pain, discomfort while exercising, and rash and blistering under my breasts. Though he did record these complaints, I did not once express dissatisfaction with how droopy my breasts were. It appears he was recording what he thought my chief complaint should be rather than hearing my experience. He also recorded my then current bra size and wrote, "patient desires to be a size." leaving my desired cup size (B or C) completely out of the notes. At my first post-operation appointment, I said to my surgeon, "so, you didn't take as much as you said you would." His response was, "yea, well I got in there and it just didn't look right. That's why it's called an estimation." During a second appointment, I indicated to his nurse that I was dissatisfied with the results. She indicated that she had reviewed my photos and said, "yeah, they're definitely lifted but there's not much of a difference in size." I responded that my intention was not to have a lift at all as I was more concerned with the size of them causing my health issues. Later, in calling his office about my frustration with my barely-reduced breasts and possible plan for revision, his nurse reviewed his notes with me over the phone saying, "he said in your most recent appointment that you still had to wear 2 sports bras to exercise... wow I'm surprised he even put that in there."

As I continued to heal, I continued to experience the symptoms I had first presented with including: daily neck pain, back pain, and headaches – despite attempting alternative methods like visiting a chiropractor, yoga, massage, using over-the-counter N-SAIDs, Tylenol and pain relief gels; and wearing multiple bras to exercise, despite buying the most supportive bra money can buy. In discussing a revision, the surgeon indicated to me that insurance "might cover" the next procedure. I indicated I spoke to my insurance company and a second surgery would be covered if medical necessity was evidenced. I spoke in detail twice with my surgeon regarding my desired results if a revision were to be completed. I tried visual comparisons and descriptive detail in hopes he would understand that I did not want to be what he called proportionate, just comfortable. At that point, I had done significant research regarding averages of tissue removed and what would need to be removed to meet my goals. I presented this to the doctor, and he responded with shock. I recall at one point he said, “so basically, you want to be tiny?” with what could only be described as a disgusted face.

When I scheduled my revision, his nurse indicated that it would not be billed through insurance because he would not be removing enough tissue and that would be fraud. I indicated that he did not remove the medically necessary amount the first time - 300g per breast was removed compared to the originally estimated 425g and medically necessary 485g - and was still billed to insurance, so it sounded as though fraud had already been committed. During my second surgery, 500g per breast was removed, more than the medical necessary amount, almost twice as much as the first surgery and 200g more per breast than estimated in my second pre-surgery consultation. If a non-professional like me could find the appropriate estimate of grams to remove, the doctor certainly should have been able to as well.

My experience hit so many issues, with not just the pain of surgery, but also the trauma related to the process of communicating my needs and being failed by my provider. My understanding of what my body needs to be healthy and comfortable has been consistent. I knew after the first surgery in which I went from an E/F cup to a DD, that my symptoms would not lessen over time. My surgeon’s approach of focusing on the visual aesthetics, ignoring my desires and goals, and believing he knew better for my body than I, was insulting and degrading.

The goals for my treatment were his own. He did not take time to consider my perspective and he believed his experience of completing "over 600 breast reductions" made him a better expert on my body than I was.

My experience was traumatizing. On more than one occasion, the surgeon indicated to me that he had done over 600 breast reductions. When I indicated my dissatisfaction, he again stated that he had done hundreds of breast reductions and only one other required a revision. My guess is, the doctor had not considered that many other women experienced the same disappointment and continued symptoms and, 1) were too afraid to say something for fear of being made to feel belittled or inferior; 2) could not afford a revision and so didn't bother to say anything; or 3) took their business elsewhere.

I did move forward with a second surgery, and it finally resulted in my desired outcome. But all I can think of is if my surgeon had listened to my treatment goals the first time, and I did not require that second surgery, I would not have had to take more time off from work, more time being unable to care for my small children, I would not have spent more time being unable to care for my small children, I would not have paid twice as much money or experienced the ongoing pain, soreness of my breast tissue, and nipple numbness. These are things I can live with – and will, since going back in time and not choosing this surgeon is, obviously, not possible.

After my second surgery, I came to the realization of how emotionally difficult the process had been. I knew I wanted to communicate my experience with the doctor, but was struggling to define where the issue lay. Then one day I was donating blood and during the initial processing, the phlebotomist asked me to show him my arms. I told him my left arm usually had the winning veins and I showed him which one has been successful. I have had several IVs and blood draws in the past couple years, and I explained to him that I had watched different nurses and phlebotomists think two particular veins would be good only to burst them time after time. At first, the phlebotomist responded that their needles were different, and it might be easier to get those veins. After some light-hearted back and forth, he said, "you know, I think it'd be pretty cocky of me to assume I know better than you about your own body. I've poked probably 6,000 arms, but I haven't poked you 6,000 times."

To be treated with dignity and respect, and with the understanding that I know my own body better than someone I had just met, showed me exactly what I was missing from the treatment I received from the surgeon.

After this realization, I sent off a long letter to the surgeon, concluding that it is demeaning and disrespectful to the women he serves to place their concerns for their physical health well below his belief that he knows their bodies better, and that women's breasts should be nice to look at regardless of how it impacts their overall health. Talk about a feminist in pink experience, in more ways than one.

When I have spoken in the past of the prospect of, and

since having the breast reduction surgery, I received a multitude of responses. Some said, "good for you," some asked that I "give them my extras," and some questioned my reasoning since large breasts are so appealing to so many. The fact that I have to defend my decision based on health and being an outlier to want to have "smaller than proportionate breasts" – according to a man who has never experienced their weight - is outrageous. On the other hand, I was able to see that many women going to a plastic surgeon likely were looking to increase the size of their breasts. I have also heard of surgeons turning to the husband pre-operation and saying, "I am going to make them look great for you."

The problem is that appearances should not just be an expectation. It certainly should not be about someone else's opinion of our appearance. Living in the world we do, it is just assumed that women are constantly trying to look better. That pressure can make you feel as though even if you are not, you should be. You should not have to feel as though you have to do something one way when it comes to how your body looks and feels.

As long as you are not hurting anyone, you should be able to do what feels best to you and for you, and still proudly declare yourself a feminist. No two people are alike, and we certainly don't fit in tiny boxes. If we listen to one another and try to find common ground, we can accomplish so much more – whether it be a comfortable breast size or an equal and just political climate.

Part Three

Human beings often have a natural tendency to rebel and struggle against the tension created by the presence of multiple truths in our lives. If we can somehow change the way we see them, if we can "let them be," surrendering to their existence and accept them into our life, we will more readily discover what they have to teach us.

- Charles Sidoti

Creating Your World

The amount of information presented here might be overwhelming. Particularly, if you are like me and tend to take everything as absolute truth, in true black-and-white fashion. When I was conceptualizing this book, my first response was, "What, so I'm never allowed to make one solid decision the rest of my life? I have to continually weigh the options forever and ever until I die? Can't I disagree with others? I can't hold firm to one belief and voice my opinion on it?"

If this is you, don't worry: that is still me some days too. I know I will continue to challenge my instincts to dive in headfirst, all-or-nothing, balls to the walls. I will continue to resist jumping to conclusions about what someone else experiences, claims, or believes, particularly if it is different from what I experience, claim, or believe. Similarly, we will spend the rest of our lives challenging the expectations that are placed on us, like the people that tell us we cannot be a feminist because we like to wear makeup.

Another way you can look at it is that you have the opportunity to take in these many, many truths to help you develop a healthy, solid view of the world; to be a feminist and believe in equality while spending the day at the spa getting dolled up for a night on the town; to believe in the 2nd amendment and the right to bear arms, and to support stricter guns laws and regulation to ensure the safety of your community members; to feel happy, sad, relieved and mad when your dad dies and not judge yourself for feeling what you feel; to consider and adopt whatever truth it is that feels most right to you, without disregarding that other people's truths are their right as well.

Go lift those weights to challenge your body and then eat a tub of ice cream if it feels right. Learn more about another culture if you feel you are disregarding somebody else's right to their beliefs. Live in a tiny house and have two storage units filled with stuff if your heart desires. Your place might be in the kitchen, but it also might be out in the world. Your place is where you want it to be; wherever you feel most comfortable and at home; where you feel genuine and authentic.

Know that your experience is real, as is everyone else's. Understand that your truth in one moment does not negate your truth in a different moment, at a different time. Focus on the *and*, rather than the *but*. Give yourself space to not judge yourself or others. Live beyond the expectations you place on yourself or others, based on some stereotype. Accept yourself and others as you are, in the moment, doing the best we all can. Ultimately, if we want to live in a world that surpasses stereotypes and prejudices, we have to create it.

My Thanks

Thank you to the women who modeled strength and courage either by shouting from rooftops or with quiet grace: my mother, Bethany Stevenson; my sister, Ashlee Stevenson; my sisters-in-law, Emily Stevenson, Cortney Dilts and Ashley Dilts; my amazing mentor, Erin King; my mothers-in-law, Joni Ankerson and Brooke Dilts and my OG Fit Mamas. Thank you to Jodiann Stevenson, Kristin Stevenson and Sophie Swedin for the passionate conversations about equality and politics. Thank you to Anna Stevenson for the ease at which she spoke of writing long-ass books which encouraged my progression and completion; for your genius suggestions, thoughts, editing and visions. Thank you to those who bounced ideas and provided encouragement. To those who reviewed my book prior to release, thank you for allowing me to be vulnerable, for being generous with your time and kind with your feedback. Thank you to Melissa Morey with Äventr Foto Co. for your amazing photography skills. Thank you to my husband, Chad Dilts for your encouragement and support, for loving my overly enthusiastic and sometimes sad self. Thank you to the parents and grandparents out there raising a feminist generation. Thank you to every feminist - female, male, black, white, straight, gay, trans, fat, skinny, and everything in between - for your daily fight for equality; during the times you feel strong, and for the times you show your vulnerability and humanity.

Photo: Melissa Morey / Äventyr Foto Co.
Print cover: Anna Stevenson

Brenna Stevenson Dilts is passionate about social equality, justice, and evidenced-based information. She graduated from Grand Valley State University with a Bachelor of Science in Psychology and from the University of Southern California with a Master of Social Work. She is now pursuing a Master of Business Administration. She lives with her husband and two young sons in a small port town, in Michigan. One of her greatest goals in life is to raise sons who are not afraid to be feminists and allies; to stand alongside women and other minorities in the fight for equality.

Made in the USA
Coppell, TX
30 October 2019

10720378R00118